"Prayer indeed is good, but while calling on the gods a
man should himself lend a hand."

Hippocrates (460 BC – 377 BC) Greek physician, the father of medicine.

The Alphabet to Successfully Selling Yourself and Ideas

Guaranteed to change your life before you reach Z

Mental health specialists agree that the anxiety of rejection
is the #1 problem plaguing the average individual. This
user-friendly book is designed to end that fear.

As simple as your ABCs

By Roland Hopkins, DKE

authorHOUSE®

AuthorHouse™
1663 Liberty Drive, Suite 200
Bloomington, IN 47403
www.authorhouse.com
Phone: 1-800-839-8640

First published by AuthorHouse 12/19/2007

ISBN: 978-1-4343-4882-1 (sc)

Printed in the United States of America
Bloomington, Indiana

This book is printed on acid-free paper.

Famous And Infamous Quotes

"Only those who risk going too far can possibly find out how far one can go."

T.S. Eliot

"Indians always succeed in their rain dance because they don't stop dancing until it rains."

Anon

"If you give a man a fish he eats one meal. If you teach him to fish he eats for a lifetime."

Mr. Limpet

"Life is not always a matter of holding good cards, but sometimes playing a poor hand well."

Jack London

"All the world's a stage and all the men and women merely players."

Wm. Shakespeare from
AS YOU LIKE IT

"Life might not be the party you hoped for, but while you're here you might as well dance."

Anon

"Ideas without action are as good as action (spinning your wheels) without ideas. NOW spelt backwards is WON. And – when someone asks you to do something and when you will get it done – you respond: "Is yesterday soon enough?"

Me

DEDICATION

Life is a succession of sales - selling us on ourselves (self-esteem) and selling others on our ideas and us. Those who learn to sell well, succeed the most. Who are the others? Unfortunately, that's most of us. Why? Because we go out of our way to avoid confrontation – the anxiety of rejection.

The American Heritage College Dictionary defines selling as: SELL (sel) v. To persuade (another) to recognize the worth or desirability of something.

And the definition of REJECT (ri-jekt') v. To refuse to accept, submit to, believe, or make use of, to refuse, to recognize and give affection to.

Think about it for a moment. REJECT is the most negative and scary word in the dictionary. Isn't there some way we can eliminate it? I say YES! So read on, neighbor.

Many self-help books have been written and published on the subject of seeking and finding success. When perusing the cluttered shelves of your favorite bookstore, which authors appeal to you the most? Donald Trump? Tiger Woods? Bill Gates? Their books are all going to be best sellers within the first week – but what can you really learn from reading their paths to success?

The truth? Between little and nothing!

Why? Because they are all unique and way beyond our reach. By the way, in our book you'll find R is for REALITY.

There is only one Donald Trump, one Tiger Woods and one Bill Gates. Did they actually write their books? Maybe yes, maybe no. Who really cares? Were their books written to actually help the readers find health, wealth and happiness? Probably not! So, why do we buy them, read half the pages and then find ourselves floundering in the same sea of mediocrity, still suffering from the anxiety of being rejected?

Am I knocking Trump, Woods and Gates? No! They are vast successes worth being idolized. Am I knocking the companies that print and promote their books? No, because it is their job to make profits for themselves and/or their stockholders.

I guess that I'm knocking all of us for dreaming that after reading Tiger Woods' book, we'll hit a golf ball 400 yards – or after reading Donald Trump's book, we'll own casinos, high-rise office buildings and host a popular reality TV show – or after reading Bill Gates book, we'll become one of the richest people in the country.

Reality tells us that none of those things are going to happen no matter how many books we read, success motivation seminars we attend or DVDs we send away for. Most of those teachers are out of everyone's reach, and sadly are more interested in our money than our success.

I recently purchased a DVD that was plugged on Oprah Winfrey's show – *THE SECRET*. Allegedly it grossed over a million dollars the first week or so. Must be good, I thought. So I watched and listened. Hmm - very familiar! Earl Nightingale recorded a 33 1/3 RPM record back in the fifties called *THE*

STRANGEST SECRET. I bought that too. Listened to it, grasped it's meaning, followed its advice and it changed my life. I actually listened to it many times over and over and still do. My anxiety of rejection went right out the window.

After about twenty minutes of *THE SECRET* and watching a bunch of experts saying pretty much what Earl had said over fifty years earlier and Socrates had preached even longer ago, I found myself wondering if the same lesson could be taught a lot easier, faster and less expensive by eliminating the exercise of the author's smiling all the way to the bank.

I spent about two seconds mulling it over in my mind and decided that YES, everyone can succeed in whatever they decide they want to seriously undertake in this free country of ours. All they have to do is figure out how to eliminate the anxiety of rejection. If that pretty gal you've been dating for the past few years says "NO" to your marriage proposal – who's the loser? She is, of course. If the boss of too many years turns down your request for a raise and you move onto another job, who loses? Your old boss, of course. This new positive attitude can be adopted by anyone willing to do the homework outlined in my user- friendly *ABC* book. I promise!

Now, if you are still with me, let's preview the *ABC* book that has been penned by a non-famous person whose only goal is to help you easily change your life. I can only assure you that everything you read here is something that you are capable of doing – and by you following the *ABC* method it will immediately change your life.

Will you get rich? Maybe! Will you be happier? More than likely! Will you live happily ever after? Indubitably! So this book is dedicated to you because you're the one who's going to do all the work with no help from Donald Trump, Tiger Woods or Bill Gates – or even Oprah Winfrey.

Ever wonder why that when you attend a sales motivation seminar for the second time you see mostly the same people you saw last year? Ever wonder why your next door neighbor, who went on a terrific new diet and paid for lots of meals being delivered to her house for several months and finally lost fifty pounds, now weighs even more than even before? Or about that guy who chewed special gum to stop smoking and is now puffing two packs a day?

I'll tell you why. Because they were looking for someone to do it for them – and that just ain't gonna happen. Ever!

If you sow, sow and sow some more for yourself, you will reap, reap and reap some more. No one is going to do it for you. Hey, if you really want to quit smoking – do it. Don't wait for someone else to do it for you. Maybe you're afraid that you'll fail if you try it yourself – the anxiety of failure!

Let's try reading a few chapters in this user-friendly book and see if we can eliminate some of that anxiety.

Hey, it's your party, so you might as well learn to dance.

Preface 1

When do we first sell? The day that we're born! And guess what? We instinctively whimper and are immediately rewarded with a soft nipple or a dry diaper. And isn't this what we do for the rest of our lives with our friends, neighbors, wives, husbands, co-workers, and most everyone we come in contact with? Isn't this what makes the world go 'round?

All of us are constantly selling (whimpering) – whether we know it or not. And those who whimper the bestest get back the mostest.

In 1962 I read a book by William Lederer entitled *A NATION OF SHEEP.* He also wrote the best seller *THE UGLY AMERICAN.* Famous guy!

The *SHEEP* book suggested that we all live in a nation of sheep ruled over by a very few shepherds. Next time you drive by a field of sheep, count them, and then find the shepherds. Usually there is only one, and he does all the thinking and leading. The sheep? They just go with the flow.

Do we live in a nation of sheep? Of course we do. And are you tired of being just one of the many sheep? Of course you are – or you wouldn't even have read this far in the *ABC* book.

The time is NOW for you to take control of your own life, and whether or not you sell yourself and ideas, or anything tangible, the *ALPHABET OF SUCCESSFULLY SELLING YOURSELF AND IDEAS* most definitely will instruct and inspire you to escape the sheep pasture and give 100% to anything you decided to undertake. Give that, and you will receive even more. I guarantee it.

Every individual learns early in life that the art of persuading others sets the stage for their personal happiness. And isn't life just that? The pursuit of happiness! By this I don't merely mean the accumulation of material goods – but that far more valuable and elusive commodity – personal self-worth. You will find that the more successful you become the more you will be in a position to help others. And if it is true that it is better to give than to receive, you will be able to give lots.

But first, try to understand and accept this concept: No one can successfully force ideas on anyone else (without a deadly weapon, of course).

Ever try to win an argument, or a fistfight? The usual result is two losers, hurt feelings, and sometimes black-and-blue eyes. This user-friendly *ABC* book will teach you how to modify your behavior, and by doing so, everyone else's. The result? No arguments! No fights! Just a bunch of winners that includes you. Especially you!

The goal in reading this book is to learn to create an atmosphere in which the other person will be comfortable doing what you want them to do, and to rid yourself of the anxiety of being rejected. Let me repeat. Create an atmosphere in which the other person is comfortable doing what you want them to do, and to rid yourself of the anxiety of being rejected.

Please don't mistake the idea of persuasion with manipulation. I am not promoting the idea of manipulating people. In my opinion, that action would come back and haunt you.

There is no one who can't benefit from learning the *ABCs* of successfully selling themselves. After all, everyone is called upon to sell – from high-powered business execs to stay-at-home moms, whose selling skills – to her kids, friends, storekeepers, her husband and his friends must be as sharply honed.

Let's face it – life is just one big sales trip. We buy, sell, and trade goods and ideas every day.

And, let's face it – that guy wearing the robe and preaches to us on Saturday or Sunday, or from the TV tube – what is he actually doing? Selling us on ideas!

Let's talk about business for a moment. Every enterprise in the world is sales-driven, and the salespeople are the stars – the brave soldiers who are getting sniped at daily on the front lines. That's why a good salesperson is in demand, can always find work, and usually is appreciated. A well-trained salesperson can sell anything. And, without good salespeople, companies go nowhere. And allow me to tell you the biggest strength of a successful salesperson. He/she is not afraid of rejection. It just rolls off their backs as they move onto the next prospect. A real good salesperson makes certain to only handle a product or service that can honestly benefit the customer. Therefore, if the customer says "NO", who lost? The customer of course! Too bad! No anxiety of rejection there – just sadness for the poor customer who will not be able to enjoy.

This book will teach you how you can be a star in your own world, big or small, selling products and services, or just selling yourself and ideas. But, with one major difference from the many, many other sales books on the market. No tricks! No skullduggery! No hocus-pocus! No fast talk, no roll up your sleeves and "I'll tell ya what I'll do for ya."

Once you have learned to sell the *ABC* way you'll puff out your chest and feel good about yourself. Why? Because through your sincere efforts, someone else sincerely benefits even more than you do - the client, friend or neighbor. Once you gain the knowledge of how easy it is to do this and how decent you feel afterwards, you will become a blessed individual who can write his/her personal and financial goal-ticket. Whatever your chosen field, something that you have to spend at least eight hours at (a third of your life), why not have fun and be the best? With these same tools you can also be successful and happy at home – 24/7.

Want to hear the premium part? As I said earlier, once you passed this course you will put yourself in a position to help someone else. You'll find yourself in a position to give. That's the key – a nondebatable reality of life. YOU CAN NEVER HELP ANOTHER UNTIL YOU HAVE LEARNED TO HELP YOURSELF.

Did you ever wonder why Mother Nature gave us two hands? Answer: One to help ourselves - the other to help someone else.

The same is true about why Mother Nature designed us with two ears and one mouth. To move forward and learn anything in life, listen twice and much as you talk.

So, is this an "INSPIRATIONAL" book or a "SALES" book? It's both! You will be inspired while learning how to succeed and shed your anxieties. And part of that success will be gaining the self-esteem to pass your message on to others. If they reject it, it's their loss. Right?

"SOW FIRST. REAP SECOND". Have you ever heard that one? My guess is that it goes back to the beginning of time and has never been changed. It's a law of "NATURE".

Write this down and never forget it: "MAN'S" laws can be broken – "NATURE'S" laws cannot.

Here's another one of "NATURE'S" laws. "GIVE" first, "GET" second.

How many people do you know who want to live life the other way? It simply does not work.

Here's one I like. "GIVE, FORGIVE and then LIVE". Print that one out and put it on your wall or refrigerator. Too many failures have tried to reverse those orders.

Fortunately for the press, man's laws are broken every day. If not, we'd have nothing exciting or devastating to read about in our daily newspapers or watch on our favorite TV news shows.

Remember, "NATURE'S" laws cannot be broken. And "SOW FIRST, REAP SECOND" is maybe the most important. The same is true for "GIVE, FORGIVE and then LIVE".

So you see this book is "INSPIRATIONAL" and also "ASPIRATIONAL".

And, as William Shakespeare so aptly said in his famous play, *AS YOU LIKE IT*, "All the world's a stage and we are just the players in it."

What did he mean by that?

He meant that the script has been written and the players (the majority of the populace) find it easiest to just go with the flow and recite the lines. But, a few of us decide to write our own play, thus control our own destiny - leave the sheep's pasture and become our own shepherds.

This *ABC* book will teach you how to be your own screenwriter and star in your own life movie or play – with a Hollywood or Broadway happy ending.

Academy Awards? Tony Awards? You'll win them all – and your supporting players will thrive in your success.

Introduction

Many of the most famous philosophers and success motivation teachers instruct that we should analyze the downside of anything before tackling it. Good idea!

What is the downside of you reading this book? There isn't one! Only upsides! I strongly suggest that you'll never again feel the need or desire to attend an expensive success motivation seminar (you may teach one). And, that alone will save you money.

Earl Nightingale says in his best selling CD, *THE STRANGEST SECRET*, "People are where they are because that is where they choose to be." If you buy his philosophy, it means that you can choose what you want to do and where you want to be as long as it is reasonable.

Nightingale also says, "The simple key to succeeding in anything is to treat your job, as minimal as it might be, as though you are the owner." That attitude sounds like a winner to me.

Here's a philosophy that you can accept now, or wait until it's too late. Life is not measured by the number of breaths you take but by the memorable moments that take your breath away. This being true, wouldn't you like to experience a few more memorable moments? So would everyone. But those who don't control their own lives have very few – and certainly don't create any.

The only downside I can think of in finishing this book (if it falls into the category of downside) is that you will be challenged to take control of your own destiny and write your own script. You will no longer have an excuse to claim that you are a victim of the elements – a trap fallen into by at least 90% of all the population (sheep). You will force yourself to accept the hard-to-accept philosophy that if you get punched in the nose, it will be because your nose was in front of someone's fist. If you refuse to accept this philosophy, you will most certainly remain on the victim's team. (PS – The victim's team always ends up in the cellar).

Hey, I'm not saying that by reading and understanding this *ABC* book that accidents won't ever happen. If one does occur, just consider it another form of rejection, a negative event that you are quickly learning how to deal with. When you have succeeded, you will no longer be afraid of rejection because you will have learned to psych yourself into the belief that you can write your own life script. Keep telling yourself that everything that happens to you is your own doing – your fault. Thus, you are able to fix it. If it is someone else's doing, you can't fix it, and you become a victim. Simple logic!

In order to grow and thrive in life you must take control of your own destiny. Look at this book as your personal guide to that goal. Don't be afraid. You have nothing to lose - and a whole new lifetime to gain.

Remember this fact: Victims can't change their lives because (in their mind) everything that happens to them is someone else's fault.

ED. NOTE: Several people who I know and are in the field of product sales, read this manuscript. In less than a year they all became number one in their company - two going on to start their own firms. Do you think they were anxious about being rejected? Actually, yes they were. But they got over it - as fast as learning their *ABCs*.

What does that tell you?

The ABC philosophy worked for them!

What did I get out of that it?

The satisfaction of lending a hand to people who successfully used it to help themselves.

When you cast aside your pride and learn to take the blame (humble) for what happens in your life, then, and only then will you be able to fix things.

Allow me to explain that in simpler terms. **IF YOU ARE NOT WILLING TO ACCEPT THE BLAME OF EVERYTHING THAT HAPPENS TO YOU, YOU CAN NEVER FIX IT.**

Are you tired of being a victim? Are you tired of being a sheep? Are you tired of being anxious of being rejected? Do you entertain negative thoughts? Are you tired of listening to your negative friends talk about doomsday?

Did you know that your greatest moments lie just ahead? And, as corny as it sounds, today really is the first day of the rest of your life?

Don't we all agree that you can't go back to the past? We can only live today - and this book will guide you in that direction.

One of the best lines I ever heard is this: "What is going to be the best day of your life?" Ask yourself that question every morning into the mirror – then answer it. Today!

May you bask in the illumination of many memorable moments.

PREFACE 2

Did you ever feel that the more things change the more they stay the same? The other day I picked up a *New York Times* from 1950. It featured articles on tax increases, promised tax cuts, stock manipulation, the New York Yankees winning the pennant, a column telling of the political and social upheaval in the Middle East, and a squib on Mike Wallace reporting something on TV. So what else is new?

This book is not about anything new. Every philosophical viewpoint contained in these pages you've probably heard or read before. Many of them can be traced back to 500 BC and earlier. I'm sure Adam would have said some interesting lines if he spoke a language. I've woven these practical philosophies together to create a fresh summary of time-tested advice and guidance. I owe my personal success to these simple principals.

Most of the sales books on the market seem to suggest tricks on how to give as little as possible for the most return. That certainly enhances "THE BOTTOM LINE". And, I'm afraid that most sales managers won't appreciate you reading this book. Why? Because very soon you will be outselling your boss, and outselling everyone else in the company. And you will also be building solid relationships with trusting customers – something many companies have never experienced before, or really cared a lot about.

But, before we get to the *ABC*'s, let's take a quick look at the origin of philosophies that are the foundation of this book.

First, three quotes from Confucius (circa 551-479 BC), one of the most famous individuals in ancient China. He said, "It is not possible for one to teach others who cannot teach his own family." In other words, work on cleaning up your own act before lending a hand to others. Or, to put it simpler: "You can't love another until you learn to love yourself." I think that thought pops up somewhere in the *BIBLE*.

Confucius also said, "The superior man is modest in his speech but exceeds in his actions." I take that to mean that humble wins and pride loses. And he said, "If you enjoy what you do, you'll never work another day in your life."

That last quote is the key to success in anything you undertake.

I recently saw George Steinbrenner interviewed by Donald Trump. George answered the oft-asked key-to-success question this way: "The key to success is to be doing something that you love."

I wonder where he got that idea.

Socrates (469-399 BC), maybe the world's most famous philosopher said, "Human excellence is a kind of knowledge. Thus, all wrongdoing is based on ignorance." Socrates knew that we all have the ability to learn from our own and other's experiences – and only by recognizing mistakes (misjudgments) and owning up to them, can we learn the knowledge to succeed.

I will explain in a later chapter why an *ABC* reader never again makes a mistake.

Jesus of Nazareth (1 AD – 33 AD?) said, "Believe and it shall be." That quote reminds me of the classic baseball movie, *Field of Dreams*. "Build it and they will come."

I just GOOGLED Jesus quotes on the internet and you would be surprised at how few there are. But, the majority of them are success-motivated. Jesus spent His too short earth-life preaching to followers on how to create an atmosphere within which people would be comfortable doing what He knew would make them happy. "Sow, reap. Seek, find. Give first, get second. Love one another. Treat your neighbor as you would like to be treated."

Dale Carnegie (1888-1955 AD), the man who taught us how to win friends and influence people said, "Take a chance. All life is a chance. People go furthest when they are willing to do and dare". And he said, "A smile always comes back."

Earl Nightingale (1912-1989 AD), probably our most famous modern success motivator said, "People are where they are because that is where they choose to be."

There is a world full of people who don't agree with that harsh statement. Unfortunately, those people continue to grovel at the bottom.

Sad! Let's face it, it is easier to stay where you are whether you are enjoying yourself or not. And to make a change may result in rejection.

Dr. Norman Vincent Peale (1898-1993 AD), the minister of the country's largest Protestant church said, "Avoid fraternizing with negative people. It's infectious."

All of these quotable people learned from each other and the earlier teachers who learned from each other - and so on. Then they all passed their knowledge onto anyone who was willing to listen and learn.

It is an accepted philosophy that knowledge is power and that ignorance is bliss.

Remember Socrates?

You can be blissful or powerful.

Isn't it comforting to know that it is your choice? That is if you are willing to learn to dare.

MY STORY - SHORT VERSION

Many years ago someone tipped me off to the fact that in the large scheme of things, compared to eternity, our lives are but a snap of a finger. The same is true of Trump, Woods and Gates. So far, the record proves that no one has yet got out of this life alive.

The moments of life are also things that you cannot save up and use later. Too bad we can't save time.

So, if you're going to accomplish anything, you better put all you got into it (100%), and enjoy it now! By the way, "NOW" spelled backwards is "WON". Let me repeat. "NOW" spelled backwards is "WON".

Here's another rule I learned early on: Never "WAIT" for anything - and certainly don't ever "WAIT" for permission to do something that will further your goals and you sincerely feel will help someone else. Build your own self-esteem to give yourself permission – the first step in taking control of your own life. In other words, most people wait for permission to succeed or fail. The philosophy in this book empowered me to give myself permission to move forward – to eliminate the anxiety of being rejected.

Do you remember Scarlet O'Hara's final lines in *Gone With The Wind?* "I'll think about it tomorrow. Tomorrow is another day." Well, my dear, sorry – tomorrow never comes. And if you wait for the right time to do something, the right time never comes.

By the way, if you followed the entire *Gone With the Wind* story, Rhett Butler didn't accept rejection and made love to her later.

Do you have something worth pursuing? Do it "NOW!"

Are you waiting for a callback on the phone? Did you make the call for a good reason? Don't wait! Call again – and again – and again. I followed that advice. It worked for me. One never knows how much time they have to waste.

Did you ever notice that there is no expiration date on your birth certificate?

When I started in business I admit that I knew nothing about sales, P & L statements, goals, or even how to balance a checkbook. My previous jobs had been as a soda jerk, bank teller, archery instructor, and disc jockey – all fun jobs, and possible successful occupations for me if I had been able to read this kind of book.

With ignorance as my guide, but knowing that I no longer wanted to be a sheep, I decided to launch a weekly newspaper.

Now, time out! Let me tell you what I did learn about starting a new business. You either find a void (and, believe it or not, there are still ideas that haven't been thought of yet), or you decide to compete against an idea already thriving. I found a void and followed some sage advice by checking the idea with some so-called experts – a man running for governor, a CEO of the second largest real estate board in the country, and a respected attorney. They all said the same thing, just like Tony Soprano - "Forget aboud it!"

"Hmm, maybe I should wait until the right time," I thought.

"Hmm, do I need their permission to start it?" I asked myself.

Lucky for me we live in a free country. If some fool with no experience wants to start a business and fall on his butt, no one will stand in his way. Not even the Lord.

Ever heard this philosophical line? "It's amazing what one can do when they have no choice."

I checked with the mirror and studied my options. I had two. I could start the newspaper and be broke, or I could do something else and be broke. Hell, I had experience in being an archery instructor, a soda jerk and a disc jockey. And, I forgot to say that in college (I never finished) I had been a gym instructor.

I now found myself (negative thinking) in a lose/lose situation.

So I did it. Raised a few dollars (not many), and within ten weeks of the inaugural issue I was broke.

Now I sorely needed answers. I readily admit that I was anxious about being rejected. "Why will some bank president talk to me?" I asked myself. "I'm a nobody," I told myself.

But, I realized that I didn't know anything about what I desperately needed to know about (a hard realization for many people). And, more than that, if I didn't learn fast, I was out of business. It's amazing what one can do when they have no choice.

So I started picking brains of business people who were successful. And, surprise to me, the bigger they were, the easier it was to get responses - as long as I acted submissive and showed respect. Yes – I quickly learned to be humble. That was the "KEY" and my first major lesson in the art of selling yourself and ideas and ridding myself of the anxiety.

"BE HUMBLE". Can you be humble? Lots of sheep can't and remain sheep all their lives.

I ate any false pride I may have owned and began learning.

One of the first things I learned is that one cannot learn anything if one already knows everything. Ever met anyone who knows everything? I think we call them, "KNOW IT ALLS." Very frustrating people who we all avoid like the plague. Try and help them out and they shut you out. And, did you ever notice that "KNOW IT ALLS" never get anywhere in life?

I've always subscribed to the theory that as soon as you stop learning, you stop growing. As soon as you stop growing you might as well write your own obituary. Even today I constantly run into people who think they know all the answers, refuse to listen to anyone offering sage advice, and continue to fail in life and wonder why. Sad!

Way back then I recall vividly that the important people that I visited felt sorry for me. I ate humble pie right in front of them. The more I asked, the more they answered, the more I listened and the more I learned.

Remember about the two ears and one mouth theory? Harvard Business School couldn't have educated me half as much. Almost overnight I was becoming a polished salesperson and newspaper publisher.

Don't get me wrong. I'm not knocking Harvard Business School – it's just that most of us will never have the opportunity to attend there.

One struggling day, driving a car that had logged ninety-nine thousand miles, two bucks in my pocket, and wearing shoes with holes in the soles, a potential client taught me a good lesson by turning the tables on me. He didn't buy an advertisement in my newspaper, but he sold me a copy of Earl Nightingale's plastic 33 1/3 RPM record, "THE STRANGEST SECRET," the only motivational record in history to ever reach gold status (one million sales).

The record taught how and why to set goals. I had always thought goals were something in hockey or soccer games. (I was a goalie in high school hockey)

I immediately began searching for more quick answers. I found them in Dale's Carnegie's book, "HOW TO WIN FRIENDS AND INFLUENCE PEOPLE," a constant big seller every year since he published it in 1936.

After reading Carnegie and mixing it with "THE STRANGEST SECRET", I attended a "PSYCHOLOGY 101" course – a class, in my opinion, every high school student should be required to pass before graduation. It taught me the value of climbing into the other person's head and looking at things from their point of view (through their eyes).

We already know what we think, so why not concentrate on what others think? That made sense to me – but no one had ever suggested the idea before – certainly not in any schools I attended.

I then proceeded in gobbling up everything I could find on success motivation.

Between picking brains, reading the masters, and applying what I had learned, I developed the number one commercial/investment real estate newspaper in the country, launched a few other periodicals, and did my share of consulting - and even had some fun along the way.

It wasn't long before people began asking me what I had done to accomplish what many had suggested was impossible. I told them about Nightingale, Carnegie, and all the other books and records I had pounded into my brain. I told them how I had picked the minds of successful people and how and why humble was important. I told them how to look at life through the other person's eyes. "Walk a mile in another man's shoes."

"You can't make people do anything," I said. "You have to try and create an atmosphere in which they will want to do what you want them to do."

"Can't be done," many told me. "You've got to get the other guy before he gets you," some insisted. "You can't run a business with the Christian ethic," more than one man said. And then too many people insisted, "The Golden Rule won't work in the cold, hard, cynical, cruel business world. He who has the gold, rules."

I didn't buy it. I was convinced that if you give, give and then give some more, it would come back ten-fold.

For me, it did!

Hey, I started out as a lowly sheep - an anxiety riddled cave man. But I was convinced that if it had worked for me, it could work for anyone. Thus, I put all the knowledge I'd gleaned from over thirty years of learning into this book.

I still don't go to sleep at night until I've learned at least one new thing that day. And let me tell you this. I have to shut up and listen real hard to accomplish that feat. When you stop learning - you stop living.

Thus, I decided to condense all of what I had learned into the easiest format I could imagine – "THE ALPHABET" – a book that allows a person to plow away all at once, or just pick the book up, open it at random, and always come away with something that can be used to further their success and give a helping hand.

Why did I pick "THE ALPHABET?" Isn't that the first thing a child memorizes? A child even learns to sing the alphabet. Can't you still remember the song? Heaven forbid - it would be humble to admit you remember it and begin humming. But isn't that how most of us learned to remember the alphabet?

How about this? We all admit that the most difficult part of any sale, whether it be to a prospect, our spouse, friend, kids

– anyone – is the close, getting someone to say yes and the fear of being rejected.

I discovered that the greatest close is a simple two words: "TRY IT!" My salespeople have been using those two magical words for over thirty years, and they have won a lot of friends and influenced a lot of people.

You try it! Try reading "THE ALPHABET TO SUCCESSFULLY SELLING YOURSELF AND IDEAS." I guarantee that it works. And if you don't think that you've learned anything significant - something you can use immediately, put the book down and grab something else - Grishem, King, Hemingway. They're all successful authors. I ought to know – I read them all, and picked their brains, too.

Have you ever heard Perry Como's popular "ALPHABET" song from the forties? (Who's Perry Como?) It ends with: "I'd love to wander through the alphabet with you and tell you what you mean to me."

I now invite you to wander though the "ALPHABET TO SUCCESSFULLY SELLING YOURSELF AND IDEAS" with me, shed your anxiety of rejection, and tell yourself what it means to you to finally be in a positive, satisfying position to help others.

Give first, and get second. Enron's Ken Ley and a bunch of other important, well-educated CEOs tried it the other way around, and where are they now?

WARNING! WARNING! WARNING! If you finish reading this book I guarantee that you will be a different person – it will change your entire life's attitudes. You will walk with your head held high, and many of your acquaintances won't even recognize you.

So, if you are satisfied with your life today, stop here. Don't waste your time reading.

But, if you aren't satisfied with your life, let's start with A.

CHAPTER ONE

Anticipate
(an-tis' a pat) adj.)

To feel or realize beforehand. Foresee.

Anticipation can save your life.

Do you like surprises?

Yeah! I do, but only on my birthday.

Do you want to live to a ripe old age successfully? Don't we all? Learning to anticipate can raise your chances. If I'd been a good student as an undergraduate, I think I would have attended law school where they teach you how to learn (anticipate) all the answers before the questions are asked. Lawyers don't want surprises in the courtroom.

A good real estate developer also learns this talent. Before presenting his ideas to a planning board, town meeting, or zoning commission, he studies all the pros and cons – learning the questions and finding answers. If he doesn't, his development will never get off the ground.

Good salespeople need to be able to have a stock answer for every question (think on their feet) – and I don't mean to be an arrogant know-it-all. They must be knowledgeable of their own product and service and what the prospect wants to know about it.

Do you know the answers?

The answers should all be contained in your presentation.

How do you know the questions?

ANSWER: By becoming the other person. Look at the topic through their eyes. Walk a mile in their shoes.

I guarantee that the more you practice this exercise, the better you will become at it.

Read the textbook, "Psychology 101". It may be the most important and underrated course taught to undergraduates. I'm sure you can find it on your local high school bookshelf, or Amazon. com.

Let's face facts - most people are only interested in what they think. Therefore, eliminate from your presentation what you think, or what you would like. Don't ever start a sentence with what you want or need or like. Why? Accept the fact that about 95% of the people you talk to don't give a damn. Concentrate on what they think and want, and put it into words.

Psychologists have proven that a person feels foolish using a rejection you have already mentioned. I try to analyze all the possible answers and rejections to a question before I inquire, discuss, or suggest.

Here's an example: I used it on my wife. "I know you like country music so I bought us two tickets to Saturday night's Toby Keith concert. And I know that baseball bores you, and I know that you like to spend Saturday afternoon horseback riding, and I know that Saturday mornings you are on the computer, etc., etc. - but someone gave me two good tickets to a Red Sox game for Saturday afternoon. I can't throw them away, and I don't want to go with anyone else but you."

How's that sound for a guy to solicit his loved one? The important part of the pitch is that I was accepting what she likes and also voicing her rejections. I didn't allow the thought of her saying "NO" to enter my mind. "You become what you believe."

By the way, she said yes.

When I'm driving my car I always think that the other vehicles might hit me. Why? Paranoid? No! Because I've accepted the fact that I can only control my own actions – not that of the other persons. When approaching a cross street, and another car is coming, I anticipate that it may fly on through.

What do I do? Common sense! I slow down and get ready to brake. Obsessively anxious? I don't think so. Just being cautious! If the car hits me and kills me, it won't be my fault. It won't go against my driving record and won't raise my insurance rate. But, so what? I'll be dead! So, I anticipate, and live.

So far, it's worked!

When is the last time you proposed marriage to a prospective spouse not knowing that the answer's going to be a positive one? I read a good proposal line recently. "Let's get married while we're still in love." I like that one.

My case rests.

Before your next persuasion attempt on anything, anticipate everything you can about the target. You already know that most people are too busy to listen to what you have to say and are only interested in what will benefit them - not what will benefit you. Sad but true!

Remember that kid who knocks on your door selling magazines? He invariably tells you that the money is to put him through college. I'm sure it's a memorized presentation. Doesn't he realize that most people don't give a damn if he goes to college? I'm sure he'd make many more sales if he could tell us the benefit we'd receive from subscribing to one or more of his magazines.

When analyzing a subject accept the fact that everyone is human first and everything else second.

EXAMPLE: (I know this is kind if deep.) A person is a human first and a woman second. A human first and an author second. A human first and a schoolteacher second. A human first and a terrorist second. And so on and so forth. Get it? All people have basic traits in common. Learn them!

We all know the old cliché that says: "All men put on their pants one leg at a time?" Well, it's true! And there are lots of things about everyone, rich or poor, man or woman, boy or girl that you can anticipate. So do it!

I know that all people like deals. So I always offer one. I don't wait for them to ask. No one has ever rejected a good deal that I know of.

All people like to be flattered. I try to sincerely compliment them. Look hard for the good points. Everyone has at least one. (I think)

Sincerely is the key word. Don't be a bullshit artist or a back-slapper. We all know those phonies and they turn us off and turn our stomachs.

All people like to hear about themselves even if they are doing the talking – so I encourage that you ask questions about them and their family or hobbies. If you can find out their passions and get them talking about those, they will immediately loosen up.

I had a haircut yesterday with a new barber. I sat in the chair and asked her one question about herself. After twenty minutes of me listening and her cutting and talking, I learned that her husband was a cop, her three kids were great golfers, she was an accomplished artist, an athlete in high school and how to color my hair in three easy lessons. When I left she still knew nothing about me, but I knew everything about her. Do you think if I had been selling something she would have bought?

"ASK AND YOU SHALL RECEIVE."

If you are dealing with a mate or friend, you should already know all those answers. I never yet learned anything listening to myself talk. Have you?

Here's some homework: Make your own list of what you think all people have in common. Use yourself as an example. You're a person. Apply this valuable information to create the atmosphere within which the other person will be comfortable doing what you want them to do and you won't be afraid to ask. You'll discover that the more you practice anticipating, the better you'll get at it.

Hey, here's an idea. Why not anticipate (vision) your idea already sold?

Earl Nightingale says, "We become what we think about". The Bible says, "Believe and be". Can they both be wrong?

CHAPTER TWO

B

Brain
(brān) n.

Intellectual power, ability, mind, intelligence. A portion of the vertebrate central nervous system that is enclosed within the cranium composed of gray matter and white matter.

You have one. Use it!

There's an urban legend that suggests that man uses no more than 10% of his gray matter. And, since we acknowledge that the brain is the greatest computer ever created, wouldn't it make sense that if we used it a bit more, we could accomplish more?

Life has been made too easy for us. Computers, golf carts, email, faxes, TV, automobiles. Hell, a person can exist today without ever leaving his house. Is this what is called progress?

But, sadly, all progressive things replace the activity of the mind. So, I say that if you shut off the TV, pull down the shades, cross your knees, and contemplate; you'll begin to feel yourself rejuvenated and mentally growing. I think it's called "MEDITATING".

Here's a test: Remove your pen and pad and write down twenty ways to improve your current situation. The first few ideas will pour out of your pen, and then you'll struggle. Everyone does! But don't stop. Dig in. Ask your brain to perform. I guarantee it will perform if you just give it a chance. Keep writing. Even write silly stuff. Just keep writing.

EXAMPLE: 1. Work harder. 2. Work smarter. 3. Finish all projects started in a reasonable time period by writing down a deadline. 4. Quit smoking. 5. Say something nice to your loved one first thing in the morning, every morning (or something nice to the first person you encounter).

Aren't all these obvious?

The listing will always become more difficult when you have to search your lazy brain. But don't give up. Keep writing! As I said, the final few will be brilliantly original because you're venturing into uncharted territory. You'll suddenly be impressed with yourself – the new you.

Don't forget this fact: For many years you've trained your gray cells to sleep and watch TV, thus they aren't in good working order. The same would be true if you stopped walking for a month. Your leg muscles would atrophy and you might have to learn to walk all over again. Most of our brain parts have been allowed to atrophy. Time to exercise them.

The more you allow yourself to think, the more surprised at how high your IQ really is. I figure that if we all use about 10% of our brains, and get by, those of us who would like to excel should attempt to ignite about one, two, or three percent more. That surely will guarantee us a place in the winner's circle.

Ever notice that in a horse race only one horse is photographed? You can be that smiling winner. Why not? And while we're talking about the brain, science has proven that people forget as fast as they learn. Did you know that statistics have shown that the average person has to hear something six times before they retain it? If that's true, if you want to get a point across, you will have to saturate the atmosphere with it. Isn't that what they do on TV? (The Geico commercial). In the world of sales, eighty percent of all transactions are made after the fifth presentation. That doesn't mean that after five phone calls when the prospect doesn't answer.

Ever hear of the drop of water on the stone theory? In a stream you find many stones worn away. Ever wonder which drop did that? It wasn't one, but all of them.

Trust me when I tell you that no one ever thought himself to death, or earned a headache from straining his natural-given intelligence.

Think and ye shall succeed. (I made that one up).

CHAPTER THREE

C

Common Sense
(kom'an-sens) adj.

Native good judgment,
common feelings of humanity.

One of the biggest travesties of justice is the fact that the most important tools we gain from school are all basically learned by the fourth grade – reading, writing and arithmetic. If the Board of Education had some common sense they'd implement a course called "COMMON SENSE" and make it a prerequisite for graduation (along with one entitled "HOW TO WIN FRIENDS AND INFLUENCE PEOPLE").

Most people have the answer to all simple everyday problems if they would stop, take ten deep breaths, and try and figure the easy way. Isn't the shortest distance between two points a straight line? I always thought so.

It doesn't take rocket science to solve most everyday problems – but just a little thought, and then action.

Some wise man once said (write this down), "The way to get something done is to just do it!" That's logical common sense if you ask me.

Another philosopher said, "The way to make a dream come true is to just wake up."

The next time someone asks you to do something, and you hear yourself say, "Yeah, I'll try", what do you think they're hearing? Common sense tells us that people who have the attitude of trying, most likely won't. Remember this line quoted earlier? "It's amazing what you can do when you have no choice."

Here's a tip: As of this moment, stop trying, wishing, waiting, and hoping to do stuff that you sincerely want to accomplish. Just do it! Don't wait for permission. Give yourself permission. Erase the anxiety of rejection. What's the downside of failure? I'll tell you. You will be back to where you started, and – so what? You'll never get to take that second step until you've taken the first one.

Do it and I guarantee that your life will immediately change, and you'll even like and respect the new you.

The next time you're confronted with a problem, big or small, step back and observe. You'll find that there are always at least two ways of doing anything – the easy way and the more difficult way.

This brings to mind a situation I ran into several years ago when I built a small guesthouse in the far corner of a property I owned. It was small, one room with a loft – but the town building inspector (after it had been 90% completed) discovered it was six feet too close to the neighbor's lot line. I received a letter from the town's attorney ordering me to either move the building six feet or tear it down. Now does that sound like any building department you've ever heard of? (Just being facetious).

I was given two choices. Both difficult! Enter common sense on my part. I used my gray cells and discovered a third choice. Very easy! I traded a piece of my land that abutted my neighbor's property for six feet of his land, which was unusable to him because it was on a steep embankment. I registered the six-foot deed and sent the town attorney a copy.

End of story!

Hey – I just used common sense. You try it next time. It works!

CHAPTER FOUR

D
Dollars
(dol'ar) n

A coin or note worth one dollar (or less),

The Bible says to tithe (give ten percent of everything you earn). Did the authors mean before or after taxes? (Just being facetious).

Earl Nightingale tells us to save ten percent of everything we earn - and let's face it, if we all had the willpower to follow that advice, we probably wouldn't need a retirement plan.

Let's look at the "dollar saved dollar earned" philosophy. Every dollar you earn is taxed. And you will frustratingly find that when you make more dollars, your taxes will balloon considerably. Every dollar you save is not taxed – thus an earned dollar might only be worth 60 to 70 cents. A dollar saved is worth a dollar. Use your common sense and figure that one out.

Sometimes it's prudent to spend less rather than make more. Or, how about doing both? That's a win/win situation. Guaranteed!

When I first made enough money to have a few dollars left over (my goal has always been to just be able to pay my bills and never owe anyone) I discovered that you have to make money for three years before you have any. My accountant told me two things that I never forgot. First: the more you make, the more you make (I had complained that I was paying too much taxes).

Second: don't ever try and fool the IRS. The few dollars you save by trying to manipulate them will never be worth the hassle, or a dollar.

I took his advice.

Don't forget this fact. Money isn't everything, but in our society you need money to buy everything. And, as comedian Steven Wright so aptly phrases it, "If you had everything, where would you put it?" Too bad those jailed and should be jailed greedy CEOs didn't follow Wright's advice.

Here's the money rule of thumb (and life's rule): "Man's laws can be broken, nature's laws cannot". Nature's law says that you have to succeed first and the money comes second.

Might sound silly and childish for me to say, but you'd be surprised at how many people attempt to skip the first step toward making money. "Give me the money first and I'll promise to work real hard second," they say. It doesn't work that way.

Over the years I have interviewed many people for jobs, and when they show more interest in how much I'm going to pay them than how hard they are going to work for me, I realize immediately that they're looking at the success equation backward.

John F. Kennedy said, "Don't ask what your country can do for you, ask what you can do for your country." Wasn't that one of the philosophies that got him elected? Let's hope it wasn't the one that got him shot.

You don't have to waste time dwelling on how much money you want to make. Your financial plan will dictate how much you have to accumulate in order to meet your obligations. But after that, succeed first and you'll make more money than you've ever dreamed of making.

I guarantee it!

Here's a PS. I just read in the "Fortune 500" that Bill Gates leads the league in income for the tenth straight year. Good for him and he deserves it, because he invented something that can benefit everyone. On the other hand, the report also revealed that the country boasted of twice as many billionaires now than five years ago. What does that tell you? I can't even fathom what a billion is. Do you know? Is it ten million? Is it a hundred million? Is it a thousand million? Ask a few people and most of them will get it wrong – just like asking them to name the Seven Dwarfs or the six Stooges.

And did you ever wonder what do billionaires do with all their money? Do they sit around and count it? Do they work their butts off to make more? Do they have two of everything? What's enough? Or not enough? I guess it's up to the earner – the person who controls his or her own life. That will be you when you finish reading this book. Not the billionaire, but the person who takes control of their own life and be able to catch up on their credit card debts. You will also be able to write your own script and dictate how much you will make. Personally, I believe you will do fine being a thousandaire.

CHAPTER FIVE

E

Enemy
(en' a-me) n.

One who feels hatred toward, intends injury to, or opposes another. A foe.

You can learn this the hard way, or take my word for it – it's impossible to make just one enemy in this world.

No matter how bad a person is; he or she always has at least one pal. Therefore, if you make one enemy (even if they deserve your rebuke and your pride tells you to punish them), you are guaranteed to lose. Sometimes it's almost impossible to be humble and bite your tongue, but in the long run, it will pay off. Better to have not earned enemies.

EXAMPLE: I walked by my sales manager's office one day and heard him swearing at one of his clients. I stopped. It wasn't like him to say a mean word to anyone. "Who the hell are you yelling at?" I asked. "No one," he answered with a chuckle. "I got peeved at this guy. So after we finished our conversation, I hung up, yelled into the phone, and got rid of all my aggressions. If he'd heard me he would've stopped doing business with us, and probably told his friends that I was a jerk. But, I feel better now that I got it off my chest."

When you discover that an individual has crossed you, it is a natural instinct to retaliate. I've always found it more prudent to fool them by retaliating with a kind act or word. That process of response shocks most people who are expecting the opposite. Maybe that's where the idea: "Turn the other cheek," came from. If you can objectively think about it, if someone did punch you and you did turn the other cheek, what would happen? You would probably get another punch or two – but then that would be it. Think about it!

I have discovered that it hurts less and you can receive the same satisfaction by writing a critical letter defaming your nemesis. But don't mail it today. Put it aside and mail it tomorrow. Ninety-nine out of a hundred times you'll never feel the need to even lick the stamp. If emailing, write the letter, press DRAFT or SEND LATER. Good for you!

I can remember an incident where my next-door neighbor went out of her way to make trouble for me with the town building inspector. It resulted in a forced sale of a small piece of my property, and me paying her an extra $5,000. She immediately purchased a new sailboat. Night after night I viewed it sitting on the bay in front of her house. I admit that the temptation was mighty strong to put a tiny hole in her bow (the boat's, not the lady's). Several of my acquaintances encouraged me to avenge. It would have been easy. I'm sure that the revenge-act would have satisfied me for at least five minutes.

Guess what? I stifled my anger and invited her and her husband to a party. I know she didn't expect to be invited. When she arrived I threw my arms around her (she'd been next door for over 25 years), and welcomed her. The bewildered look on her face was worth much more than my possible few minutes of revenge had I sunk her boat.

And maybe that's where the cliché "KILL THEM WITH KINDNESS" comes from.

I could relate more incidents where I pulled the same turn-the-other-cheek trick on clients and neighbors. In my opinion, they were all real jerks and deserved to be punished. But I humbly killed them with kindness, and probably won nine-out-of-ten games. That's a better average than those $15 million a year baseball pitchers.

The same philosophy works financially in business as Sam Walton proved with his Wal-Mart attitude - service, service and more service. The client is always king – always right even if he's wrong. The best thing to do is to bite your tongue, eat your pride, and quietly accept his check.

Isn't that really the plot of all businesses? Figuring out an honest way of getting the money from their checkbook into yours.

Sam Walton decided that he would compete against all the successful discount stores by offering service while still offering low prices. They had succeeded years earlier by offering no service and low prices.

It worked then for them!

Sam's new policy worked for him and millions of shoppers.

The stubborn discounters refused to change their policies or turn the other cheek. All soon went out of business.

I can recall Dunn & Bradstreet calling on me many times and offering to sell what they termed a "MUST" assistance. They were peddling a service wherein they ran a credit check on each customer before my company accepted the business. Nice help!

I asked them why I needed that information (dumb question!). Don't forget, back in those early days I knew nothing about business. They answered: "No one would ever want to do business with someone who had bad credit." Smart answer and I'm sure the right answer.

They probably thought I was crazy, but I said that just because the client didn't pay someone else, I didn't think that necessarily meant they wouldn't pay me.

What the hell did I know?

They suggested that I should at least make the new client pay up-front the first time he bought an ad in my newspaper. (Good business practice – maybe taught at business school). But, nope, I never had the luxury of attending business school. I was forced to be educated from the "School of Hard Knocks" better known as "LEARN BY DOING". At that institution they teach "COMMON SENSE" and "HOW TO WIN FRIENDS". Thus I told D & B that I wanted my new clients to get in the habit of receiving a bill from me every month just like the phone bill, electric bill, the rent bill, etc. When they were licking the tasty stamp on their necessary bills - I wanted them to see my invoice and make it a custom to pay that one, too.

The ultimate result was that I trusted a lot of clients who might have been slow - or maybe even stiffed others. But, believe it or not, some of my best customers turned out to be people who I know for a fact that D & B would have presented me with documented evidence not to do business with.

There is a moral to that story. If you treat someone a certain way, often they become the way they are treated. If you tell your kids every day what a slob they are because their room is a mess, most likely they will become slobs with messy rooms. If you continually accuse someone of being a loser, most likely they will become a loser. Maybe that's why Dr. Norman Vincent Peale wrote the "POWER OF POSITIVE THINKING".

The worst enemy you can ever have is yourself if you allow negative thoughts to seep into your brain. Remember the cliché: "Be careful what you wish for because your wish might come true."

I knew a woman who became paranoid about someone breaking into her street-floor apartment. She couldn't get it out of her brain. She didn't wish for it to happen, but she constantly feared it happening – thinking about it all the time. Yup! You guessed it! It happened! Police psychiatrists say that the intruder picked up on her negative energy waves and something drew him to her address. The perp couldn't explain it.

Never underestimate the power of your brain waves.

Ever wonder how the Pyramids in Egypt were built? No one really knows for sure. But there is a school of thought that says a bunch of smart Pharos sat around, concentrated together and mentally moved those large blocks. There's a name for that. Telekinesis.

Over the years I trained myself to think only positive thoughts about every new client, and in over thirty years of billing history I've been proven over ninety-five percent right.

Hey, by allowing them to advertise in my newspaper I helped them to succeed, which ultimately helped them to be able to pay the bill. (Common sense!)

It takes a humble person to turn the other cheek. I've discovered by trial and error that humble wins and pride loses. Remember the race between the tortoise and the hare? Who wins every time? Not the arrogant hare – but the humble tortoise.

There's a reason why "PRIDE" is one of the "Seven Deadly Sins". No one can ever get anywhere using it as a tool, and you can't eat it, wear it, or live in it. And, it's hard enough to succeed in our competitive, cruel world without creating unnecessary enemies - especially ones you don't even know about. The opposite is also true. The best advertising one can enjoy is by doing a good turn for someone else. They'll always tell their friends. That positive action will lead to you making new friends – maybe ones you don't even know about.

What's that cliché about a friend in need ---?

CHAPTER SIX

F

Fun

(fun) n.

A source of enjoyment, amusement, or pleasure.

Isn't life supposed to be "THE PURSUIT OF FUN?" The American Heritage College Dictionary defines "FUN: A SOURCE OF ENJOYMENT, AMUSEMENT, OR PLEASURE". You knew that. Everyone knows what fun is. But how much time do we have for "FUN"?

You don't have to be an ace mathematician to count the fun moments in a day. Our short lives are made up of many moments. How many of them are memorable? What if I asked you to tell me something you remember back when you were six, seven, eight, nine or even twelve years old? My guess is that unless your parents took you to Disney World, or you experienced something violent, you'd probably draw a blank. The answer might be that you couldn't recall any memorable moments.

What about last year?

Isn't that sad?

Life is not measured by the number of breaths you take, but by the memorable moments that take your breath away. I don't know who said that, but isn't it the truth?

I figure that we all spend about eight hours a day sleeping, eight hours on necessary incidentals (primping, shaving, washing, eating, driving to and from work, etc.). Some of you might disagree and say that it is during the latter eight hours that you find time for fun – so I suggest that period is limited. Okay? The other eight hours (or more) is spent at your place of employment. That adds that up to twenty-four.

I did pass math in school.

Nothing we can do about the eight hours sleeping, unless we can learn to script our dreams.

Not much we can do about expanding the incidental eight, unless we stop eating, washing, and brushing our teeth, or move into our office.

That leaves the eight that we work.

How many people do you think have "FUN" at their jobs? Ten percent? That may be high.

A national survey showed that up to eighty percent of people would change vocations if they had a chance.

Obviously we have little authority over the other sixteen hours, but we do have control over where we work and what we work at.

I recall a close friend who admitted over a few beers that he hated his job. But, he had three children to get through school, a mortgage and a wife he didn't care much for. His responsibilities led him to eight hours a day of employment that he abhorred.

One sunny summer Sunday, right in front of all his neighbors, he dove into the ocean and never came up.

I hate that story, but it's true.

Common sense answer would have been for him to give himself permission to find a job he enjoyed. However, he would have been first forced to build up his self-esteem and cancel the anxiety of failing and dealing with not being able to afford his expensive life style - and be willing to start over.

Scary!

Easy to say, difficult to accomplish - especially approaching middle age. He chose another path.

But, just maybe if he had been able to read this book when he was just starting out in the world of opportunity, he would have chosen a different field of endeavor – one he had passion for. Or just maybe if had been able to read this book later in life, he would have been able to look at himself in the mirror and say, "I know I can, I know I can, I know I can."

One of the categories that everyone can be placed into is the enjoyment of receiving a bargain. I've never met anyone who didn't love a deal – even those billionaires. They still put on their pants (or panties) one leg at a time.

I remember one of my first "BIG" sales. It was to a large lumber company who owned lots of real estate. I proudly sold them a yearly advertising package plan for a big one thousand dollars.

"What are you going to charge us?" they boldly asked me.

I mulled the question over in my newly educated mind, bright enough to realize that even though they were very rich, they were looking for a deal.

"How about eight hundred," I sheepishly said

I bounced back to my office and told everyone how I'd sold a thousand-dollar account for eight hundred.

I was happy!

A week later I discovered that they'd bragged to their boss about how they'd beaten me out of two hundred.

They were happy!

I guess there are at least two perspectives to every story.

I always allow my salespeople to give a nice bargain. "Offer it, and everyone will be happy," I said and assured them that it's fun to see happy people, and fun to create an atmosphere in which people become happy.

I also know that a good salesperson gets a thrill when completing a sale. Thus, if I can set up lots of sales opportunities for a salesperson, they're going to have more fun (memorable moments).

I can't imagine being a salesperson of forklifts or river barges. How many deals do you think those guys close in a week? Or even in a year? Not enough fun there! Obviously, one commission on a crane is probably more than two hundred sales made by my salespeople, but some of my staff score several times in a single day.

Sounds like fun to me.

Kobe Bryant always has a smile on his face. I mean for sinking baskets.

If you're not having fun where you are now employed, write down ten things that you'd rather be doing. Or even five. Or how about one? Study the list. Maybe you can fit into another field without as much hassle as you anticipate. Think about T.S. Eliot's famous quote: "Only those who risk going too far can possibly find out how far one can go."

I guarantee that you'll excel easier at what you enjoy and it's certainly worth the exercise. Then go for it. Don't "TRY", don't "WAIT", and don't get "PERMISSION" - just do it! Erase that damn anxiety feeling of being rejected. From now on, those who reject you are the losers. With that new attitude you will become a winner. I guarantee it!

If I'd had my druthers at age twenty-one, what would I have attempted? I wanted to play shortstop for the Boston Red Sox. Great dream! But, I never batted over .250 as the leadoff hitter for the Waban Eagles in the Newton Twi-League. I still have my warm-up jacket won for being city champs. I share it with the moths, but will never throw it away. The season was too much fun and produced too many memorable moments. (They don't make jackets that last fifty years anymore).

You're career goals must be realistic. But, I know now that if I'd really wanted to be in baseball, I'm sure I could have become a sporting goods salesman, a coach, a PR man for a professional team, or any number of other jobs allied with sports. Once the will is there, the whys and wherefores take care of themselves. You become what you believe and dare to do.

Frankly, I didn't know what I wanted to do and that's how I ended up with something I knew nothing about, then was forced to learn real fast. What's that line again about being surprised at how much you can accomplish when you have no choice?

So, you see, it's ultimately up to you.

Fortunately, you live in a country where you can enter any field of endeavor. No one will stop you. Your choice! And also your choice on how high you rise, and the pleasurable moments that go along with it.

If you want to have some fun give yourself permission to get the hell out of that job you hate, a lousy relationship, cold weather – or whatever you're doing that turns you off. Get into something that turns you on 24/7.

Stop thinking about it an do it!

CHAPTER SEVEN

G

Golden
(gol' dan) adj.

Of the greatest value, important, precious.

The "GOLDEN RULE" reads: "HE WHO HAS THE GOLD – RULES".

No! That's not it. Only fooling! It's: "DO UNTO OTHERS AS YOU WOULD HAVE THEM DO UNTO YOU."

However, in reality, the "GOLDEN RULE" is a powerful standard that very few follow. As a matter of fact, as the population of the world grows, it becomes more mystifying. Fewer people are even able to quote "THE GOLDEN RULE."

Here are a few facts and figures to dwell on.

The United States reported over eleven thousand gun deaths last year. Great Britain admitted to 64, Canada 45, and Japan 39.

In the USA no one is able to figure out how to communicate with his neighbor. Did you know that The United States leads the world in litigation? Are we proud of that record? I don't think so.

Is it true that one of the oaths that lawyers take is to seek the truth? In what courtroom do they practice that activity?

If you'd like to succeed you will find that the "GOLDEN RULE" rules. In sales it is: Do unto your prospect as you would have him/her do unto you.

In a relationship it is: "Do unto your partner as you would like him/her to do unto you." Simple? Common sense?

Think! Anticipate! What does my neighbor want? Okay, I'll give it to him or her. If I'm right, I can make a deal because I'm going to offer it before he or she even asks. No dickering, no negotiating, no chiseling.

Let's talk about who you choose to do unto – and it should be your choice. In sales you select who can best benefit from your service or product. If you do that well enough, believe in yourself and your service or product and select the right people to present it to - you will succeed. Guaranteed!

Remember, you have to sell yourself on yourself before you can sell anyone else – so let's analyze you.

Up until now you have made many mistakes in your life – probably traveled the same road over and over – and planning to continue following it even though you know by now that it leads nowhere.

As of this moment you are going to eliminate the word "MISTAKE" from your vocabulary. Why? Because it is too negative! It denotes too much negative energy, and enough "MISTAKES" lead to rejection.

On the other hand, even billionaires occasionally make misjudgments. From this moment forward, when you slip up, it is a "MISJUDGMENT" and not a "MISTAKE".

Remember your school days? What did the teacher do when you had a bunch of mistakes on your tests? You flunked! But, on the other hand, if you had humbly visited the teacher's office after a poor showing and pleaded misjudgments, you might have even been given another chance. (Here's the rule: "Self-esteem people don't make mistakes – but an occasional misjudgment.") Copy that?

If by chance you follow this positive advice and do strike out, you'll move onto the next neighbor.

Yup! You're going to begin to treat your neighbor like you would like to be treated. And by doing that you will end up with the gold. That's nature's rule. Remember – "NATURE'S RULES CAN'T BE BROKEN."

CHAPTER EIGHT

H

Hearing
(hir' ing) n.

The sense by which sound is perceived.

Why don't people always do what they're told? Maybe sometimes it's because they didn't understand what was related to them. When we watch those popular legal shows on TV we see that there are at least two sides to every story. If ten people witness an accident, or murder, you hear up to ten different narratives. Therefore, understand that you can control what comes out of your mouth, but not what goes into someone else's ear. Allow me to repeat. It isn't what you say to someone, it is what they hear you say - and sometimes that can be completely different.

Here's where the correct analyzing of the other person comes into play.

A sincere compliment usually gets someone's concentration. Believe it or not some people have a listening attention span of less than twenty seconds, and will never admit it to you or even to themselves. Pseudo pride! I employed one excellent salesperson that began losing clients because he'd print their newspaper ads over and over without their permission. He'd suggest that they run every week or once a month. They'd buy the ad, maybe say, "run it twice then check back with me". He would only hear the first twenty seconds and not their instructions. After dealing with several irate customers his wife finally admitted to me that his listening attention span was about twenty seconds. From then on I made him write everything down, and also mail the agreement to the client.

If you want to stay in control, always check to make sure the person you're talking with, whether it be someone in your personal life or a sales prospect, understands what you are saying. If it's something that you feel is important enough, as you explain it, hand it to them written on a piece of paper, or email it to them. That way they will use two senses – ears and eyes. Place the onus on you – not on them to make sure they perceive what you perceive.

Speaking of the onus, here's a business tip that many bosses don't like to hear or adhere to. "It isn't just knowing the product or service that equals success in a business – it's knowing how to treat your employees."

I always suggest that the salesperson should try and treat his fellow employees at least as well as he treats his clients.

Makes sense to me!

I strongly suggest that bosses do the same. In other words, the onus is on a "good" boss to schmooze the employees – not the other way around.

Why?

Think about it. The employees can find another job at the same pay in a heartbeat. Can you find another job with the same pay that easily, Mr. Big Wheel, highly compensated boss?

I don't think so.

Turn up your hearing aid and make it work for you. If you encourage the other person to talk, they will divulge themselves. Cherish the person who reveals their wants. They save you the trouble of seeking those important answers.

Learn to shut up and listen. Isn't that why Mother Nature blessed all of us with two ears and only one mouth? To listen twice as much as we talk.

Here's a thought: Did you ever learn anything listening to yourself talk? Think about it the next time you're flapping your tongue and trying to sound important.

CHAPTER NINE

I
Increase
(in-kres') v.

To become greater or larger.

A successful person either goes forward or backward. Either increase or decrease. As the great black baseball pitcher Satchel Paige once said, "Don't ever look behind you because someone may be gaining on you."

So much for the guy who works hard, finally makes it, is satisfied with his lot in life and then decides to stop growing.

One can always move forward without backbreaking effort. The key isn't working harder, longer, or even faster. It's to teach yourself to work smarter. Be fully aware of where you are and then plan at least one positive action each day to move yourself forward. Learn at least one new thing every day. (Of course, if you already know everything, you can't ever learn anything new).

If it gets to be five PM and you haven't learned anything yet, panic.

I sincerely believe that when a person stops learning, they stop living. And when you stop living and your heart still beats, what have you got?

Visited any nursing homes lately?

You got up this morning, which should have been your first clue that you have enough health to dance. It really doesn't make any difference how old you are since we all can only live one day at a time - whether we are twenty-five or eighty-five. Yesterday is the past and tomorrow may never come. By the way, tomorrow you'll say it's today.

I remember a bar frequented by college kids back in Hartford, Ct. in the 50's. The barroom displayed a large sign behind the bar that said: "FREE BEER TOMORROW". I can't tell you how many times we attended waiting for tomorrow to come.

It never did!

The sign always read the same.

So much for what we learn in college and how smart we were.

I'll let you in on the "MOST POSITIVE THOUGHT" that you can carry in your head.

Ready?

QUESTION: What will be the best day in your life?

ANSWER: Today!

Don't forget that - and don't forget to tell yourself that phrase in the mirror every morning when you are grooming yourself. "THE BEST DAY OF MY LIFE IS GOING TO BE TODAY."

Learn something everyday!

Do something positive every day!

As ye grow so ye will go. (I made that one up).

CHAPTER TEN

I

Imaging
(im'l-jing) n.

The use of mental images to influence bodily actions.

It may seem like magic, but anyone can learn the art of imaging. A developer looks at a piece of land and images a beautiful building rising out of the ground.

When you were a teenager you looked at that young, cool new person on the block and imaged a date (and maybe more) with that person.

He who images best finds his dreams come true.

The greatest test is to image a parking space up closest to where you are going. If you do it hard enough, invariably a space will be there waiting for you. Why? Magic? No! Here's the trick. (Isn't there always a trick?) Most people figure it's a waste of time to drive all the way to the front and haven't read this book yet. Remember, you are shedding the anxiety of failure-fear and becoming the one-in-ten that succeed. That means that only one in ten will drive all the way up to the front and look for the open space.

Do the math!

The Indians dance until it rains. They call it the "Indian Rain Dance". They image themselves soaking wet – then it eventually happens.

In my business I found it prudent to "IMAGE" what a newspaper page would look like. I'd tack it to my wall in front of me; draw the empty ad spaces (grid), leaving the remainder for stories. I'd do this for the entire paper. I'd be able to tell you exactly how many ads would be sold, and how many stories would appear on Tuesday for a newspaper that didn't go to press until the next Monday. Other newspapers allowed (and still allow) ads to dictate their size.

I did it the opposite way.

Why?

I didn't know any better.

How?

By imaging.

The psychology of it proved to be that a person could only stare at a hole for so long before they had to fill it in.

If you discovered a big hole in your back yard, how long would you stare at it before every bone, muscle, brain cell, and instinct in your being would force you to fill it in?

I rest my case.

A successful shopping center developer will tell you the same thing. He places an architect's drawing of all the stores on the wall and gives himself permission to decide who'll tenant them. When he's done that positive exercise with his imaged approach, he politely and tactfully informs the prospective tenants.

You can follow the same plan. Image your desire, and then image yourself already having it.

An acquaintance of mine clipped a picture of a new boat out of a magazine and placed it on his wall. Within six months he owned one just like it.

Another acquaintance secretly tacked a picture of an attractive lady on his wall. Within a month he was dating her. Once he had imaged himself with her, she had no chance. (I never told her this story and wonder if she's reading this book and recognizes the event. Oops!).

Practice your imaging. My experience says it is like magic, and it works every time.

WARNING! WARNING! WARNING!

Imaging used sincerely and correctly is a powerful and proven force. Be careful not to use it for practical jokes that might back-fire and hurt someone, or for anything evil. I have also seen it work with dangerous results.

I think I'll keep those stories to myself – especially the time when I stuck some pins into a toy voodoo doll and wrote some-one's name on it. The result wasn't funny.

CHAPTER ELEVEN

J

Judge
(juj) v.

Form an opinion or estimation
or after careful consideration.

It says in that black book found in most every hotel and motel room (the best-seller that so many of us never look at), "Judge not yet ye be judged." Ever wonder what that really means? It means that you can spend a lot of wasted time and energy judging other people, and since no one is perfect, it doesn't take very long until you find their faults.

Good for you!

What does it prove when you discover someone else's imperfections?

Nothing!

On the other hand, if you spend the same energy seeking someone's good points (almost everyone has a few - I think), your life will be much happier, and so will theirs.

This reality-fact is more important than you realize. If you are a "JUDGER" of negativity, it can eventually paralyze any future you have working for someone else, or even working for yourself.

I have a friend who found it unfeasible to work for anyone else because she always detected that the people around her were inferior. She was a grade "A" worker, but bounced from job to job, always judging her bosses and fellow employees.

She finally launched her own company, soon discovering that she couldn't keep anyone working for her because they were all inferior (in her mind).

She had certainly unearthed a lonely path to failure.

Learn this: "Never compare anyone to yourself. If they were as talented and as smart you are, they would be vying for your job."

Here's a major key to opening the people-acceptance door. When you meet someone, immediately look for something positive about that person. It may be their appearance, their clothes, their hair or something you know that they accomplished.

Seek and I guarantee you will find something, no matter how small.

Make it a point to "SINCERELY" compliment at least one person every day. Then watch your remark light up their face.

Is there anything wrong with bringing some happiness into someone else's life? It's a win-win situation. You'll feel better for creating an atmosphere in which they feel better.

That seldom looked-at black book also suggests that we all will be judged on our final day.

I can wait!

I have a lot of things to accomplish before judgment day.

How about you?

CHAPTER TWELVE

K

Kennedy

(ken'i-de)

The 35th president of the United States (1917-1963) Assassinated in Dallas, Texas, November 22, 1963.

Remember him?

You're supposed to pick brains of people who know stuff. Right? What did we learn from John F. Kennedy? How to woo Marylyn Monroe? Not really, but it made good "National Enquirer" reading.

A young, handsome, charismatic John F. Kennedy was elected president in a period when the country desperately needed a dynamic youthful person to lead. Even though he only served three years, his shortened term is remembered by all.

Where were you the day Kennedy was shot? Many of you weren't born yet. But those of us who were, we know exactly where we were and what we were doing at that moment.

If you weren't born yet, ask anyone who was and I guarantee they will tell you exactly what they were doing at that moment.

Interesting!

K is for Kennedy because he said this: "Ask not what your country can do for you; ask what you can do for your country." That's a very important sale's point. Don't think in terms of what the other person can do for you (that's what all your competitors are already doing); think of all the ways you can serve, then inform your prospect or friend or mate. In this guise, you're not being a salesperson (dirty word); you're just a messenger.

I don't have any people labeled salespeople working for me. I call them publishers. It makes them feel good to be called a publisher, and it creates an atmosphere in which the potential client feels important talking to a publisher.

Here's what I teach my publishers: If you truly believe in yourself, and your product, or service - and you have dilengtly created a prospect list of those who can benefit from whatever you are selling, then you can honestly say this: "I am not trying to sell you anything, but I am just informing you of something that I sincerely believe can help you."

This approach places you in the position of being a trusted messenger, not an average salesperson who we all feel is only interested in pushing a product so he or she can make a commission.

I guarantee that you'll be surprised at how well this soft but positive-sell works, and how quickly your sales figures grow.

PS – Don't tell your sales manager. He most likely hasn't read this book and was taught just the opposite approach.

PERSONAL STORY: In the late eighties (Reagonomics), I ran a daylong sales seminar for a major northeast publishing company. I strongly suggested the following approach: "Spend time analyzing what you can do for your prospect - what's the most you can offer your prospect for the least return to you. I guarantee that over a period of time it will come back ten-fold."

You should have seen the disapproving expressions on the three greedy partner's faces who stood in the back of the room glaring at me. I had been labeled as "the father of commercial real estate newspapers," so they thought I had the secrets to success.

I did, but they couldn't grasp it.

The next week one of them phoned me and said that four of his salespeople had quit. When I asked why, he admitted that the salespeople loved my approach and wanted to use it in their sales. He refused! They resigned! So much for them paying me to instruct their sales staff.

Here's the kicker. Two years later, at the beginning of the Great Recession, (remember 1989 – 1991) his company died. I wonder if he would have survived if his salespeople had been given a free hand to do what I had suggested – kiss the client's butt with a sincere smile.

My company persevered by following the same philosophy we had always practiced. "GIVE FIRST, GET SECOND."

Kennedy is also remembered for this quote:

There are three kinds of people.

1. Those who make things happen.

2. Those who watch things happen.

3. Those who wonder what's happening.

Which one are you? Or going to be soon?

CHAPTER THIRTEEN

L

Listen

(lis'an) v.

To make an effort to hear something.

Mother Nature gifted us with two ears and one mouth. Wonder why? To listen twice as much as we speak. Remember that fact the next time you want to break into someone's conversation to put in your two cents worth. (Inflation has ballooned that figure up to at least two dollars – or more). One of the greatest compliments I ever received came after spending an afternoon with a successful salesman. He said, "You know, Rolly, we spent all afternoon talking and I don't know anything about you."

"But I know all about you," I said.

I did! And that has happened to me many times. I listen, and when the prospect stops talking, I encourage them to continue. I keep asking questions. I've learned that all people like to hear about themselves, even if it's coming out of their own mouths. It's a law of nature. (And if you are taking copious notes – "NATURE'S LAWS CAN'T BE BROKEN." I let them talk and talk. Then I learn and learn.

"Ask and you will receive." Always remember that line, "If you give a man a fish he will eat one meal. If you teach him to fish he will listen and never go hungry." That's not the exact line, but it means the same.

EXAMPLE: Many years ago I had the occasion of calling upon the mayor of a major city. I waited and waited. As I waited I studied his office for some tips on what made the mayor tick. That information might tell me where his interests lie, or anything else about him I could glean before I attempted to "SELL" him something. Usually you can discover personal traits about a person by the pictures on the wall, or desk, or the books in his bookcase. However this prospect turned out to be a rare bird – his desk was squeaky clean, no pictures on his wall and no bookcase. Maybe a neat freak?

Attention all you salespeople and wannabe salespeople. Here's an important tip on confronting anyone for the first time. Punch in the person's name on "GOOGLE.COM." You'll be surprised at what you might learn.

Back to my mayor story that happened long before they had invented the Internet.

There was one item on the top of his desk that stood out. A baseball! Just a simple horsehide baseball! (Do they make baseballs out of horsehide?)

A few minutes later the mayor rushed in, apologized for being late, and abruptly asked me what I wanted. I figured I had about thirty seconds (if lucky) to pitch my wares.

"Baseball fan?" I asked with a friendly grin.

He shot back an equally wide smile, and we proceeded to talk about the Boston Red Sox for the next half-hour. Needless to say, whatever I was selling, he bought. Anything incredulous about me immediately disappeared.

About a month later, coincidentally, I happened to see him walking down an aisle in Fenway Park.

"Hello Mayor Harrington," I greeted.

"Oh, hi Rolly," he said and waved back.

I guess he had listened to my name.

TIME OUT!

They have halftime in football, seventh inning stretch in baseball, breaks between acts in a stage play and even recess in school.

Science has suggested that the average person can retain ten percent of what they hear for the first time. That being true, and all of us are considered at least being average or above (whatever that means) should probably review what we have already learned ten percent of.

Did you ever notice that when you were in school, one person stood out and received between 90 and 100 (A's) on all tests? Did you ever wonder why? We all assumed it was because he or she was brilliant and had it made. Why couldn't we measure up even after an all-night cramming session? I recall an "OPEN-BOOK" test that I scored a C on.

I did some investigating and found out that most of those students who received all A's had a photographic memory. They couldn't help doing well. They read the lesson once and it stuck in their minds.

You and I couldn't possibly compete with them in academics, but what about now?

I'll tell you what about now. This book will put you way past them in everything you do.

Why?

Let's review.

A – ANTICIPATE. Get good at that and you will approach being psychic.

B – BRAIN. Don't sell yourself short. Learn to use yours. Work smarter not harder. "As ye think so ye shall succeed."

C – COMMON SENSE. Most of us try to do things the hard way and don't seem to finish what we start. Not anymore!. We're going to use our common sense. We were all blessed with it.

D – DOLLARS. While we agree that money can't buy happiness, common sense tells us that happiness can't buy money. And just because it's only made of paper and meant to be spent, we're going to figure out how to save at least ten percent of all that we earn. A penny saved is a penny earned no matter how you look at it.

E – ENEMY. We know that any fool can find someone else's faults. We're going to look for the good points and cease making enemies. Hate is a wasted emotion and only hurts us. Start loving yourself first and your neighbor second. In other words, you cannot love anyone else until you have learned to respect (love) yourself.

F – FUN. There are only twenty-four hours in a day. Eight are spent sleeping and another eight on incidentals. That leaves eight more. What we do with those eight drives our lives. Might as well find something that brings us enjoyment and make a living doing it. Give yourself permission to do something you're passionate about and see what happens.

G – GOLDEN RULE. I always thought that the more you take, the more you get. But I guess I was wrong. It appears that the more you give, the more you get back in return. Food for thought!

H – HEARING. Apparently it isn't what you say that counts; it's what someone hears you say. More food for thought!

I – INCREASE. Once you commit yourself to going forward in life, you can't stop. So you just keep moving like that little bunny on TV. PS – TIP: Don't start a task unless you intend to finish it.

J – JUDGE – Don't ever measure people by you. Be glad that you're better than they are and stay that way – but don't tell them. Keep it our secret.

K – KENNEDY – He must have had something special if we're still talking about him. He said that there are three kinds of people - those who make things happen, those who watch things happen, and those who wonder what's happening. Which one are you? Which one are you going to be when you finish reading this book?

L – LISTEN – Mother Nature gave us two ears and one mouth. I wonder why? Maybe to listen twice as much as we talk? I never learned anything listening to myself talk. Did you? Shut the hell up and listen. Maybe you'll learn something. Remember this: "All people enjoy hearing nice things about themselves – even if the words are coming out of their own mouth." Encourage them to talk about themselves.

END OF BREAK

How's your anxiety of being rejected? Better? Good!

BACK TO WORK

CHAPTER FOURTEEN

M
Motivation
(mo' ta-va' han) n.

To provide with incentive, move to action, to impel.

One of my pet peeves is a "Success Motivation" seminar. While I admit that everything taught is sound and the teachers are well motivated – about ninety-five of the attendees are there for one purpose – to see if the instructor can show them how to accomplish something without the student having to do anything. Next time you attend a Motivational Seminar look around and see how many faces you recognize from last year. You'll see many of the same faces attending again, hoping that the teacher will do it for them.

How does one quit smoking? Get hypnotized? Wear a patch? Maybe if you wore a patch over your mouth. No! The only way one quits smoking is to decide to quit smoking – want to do it – and then do it. Not wish, hope and then attend a "Quit Smoking" seminar that always helps the instructor get rich.

The same is true about losing weight. Many people go on the latest fad diet and lose weight. Then what happens? How many of them gain it back? Most of them. Why? Because they're relying on the instructor to do the work for them. Then they buy into the latest, expensive gimmick-crutch to lose weight. What happens? They lose weight again.

How about an answer? Not Atkins. Not Pritikin. Not Richard Simmons. I have the best diet that can't fail and it won't cost you anything to follow it. I won't even send you a bill like all those con artists on TV and on the web who suggest that they have something that will allow you to live to a hundred, get you all excited and then tell you that you have to send away for the information. Is that called bait, switch?

On my diet you don't need an instructor, or any special food. You don't have to watch VCR or DVD tapes, read books, study labels, or count calories.

Here it is. Send me a thousand dollars. ("Only kidding!)

Here it really is: "THE CAN'T MISS DIET." Just eat half of everything put on your plate. Understand? Eat only half of what's put in front of you.

Remember when your mother used to tell you to clean your plate? (My mother was way overweight and if I didn't clean the plate, she cleaned it for me with her fork.)

I hate to suggest that you disregard your parent's advice, but forget what your mother taught you about emptying your plate. I highly suggest that you garbage the second half of it.

By the way, this simple and free diet has never failed anyone who stuck to it, and you can eat half of everything you love.

PS: Watch your carbs. Don't cut them out – cut them down.

Getting back to all the despondent people who attend the "Success Motivation" seminars. Ever wonder who succeeds and makes the money? The instructors, of course. They drive away in their priceless cars, or fly home in their expensive jets, while you either thumb home, or jump-start your rickety, twenty-year-old Honda Civic.

What's wrong with this picture?

You're what's wrong. Don't blame the instructor. Everything they tell you is true. I guarantee that a few of the people listening will follow the instructions and change their lives. But ninety-five percent won't. They'll run into the office everyday for about two weeks full of piss and vinegar, and follow all the instructions on the notes they took while at the seminar. They'll even listen to a few of the CDs they were coerced into buying. But, too soon, they'll realize that what they witnessed wasn't magic. The instructor wasn't going to do the work for them.

Just like the hypnotist isn't going to slap the cigarette out of your hand or food off your plate when you finally succumb to temptation.

Did the Lord slap the apple out of Eve's hand? No, He didn't – to the downfall of all of us.

Here's my advice. Go to one seminar. Listen! Buy the recordings. Faithfully use your automobile radio CD player as a college. If you're a half-hour from the office, you'll get an hour of motivation lectures a day, five hours a week, adding up to 240 hours a year. It certainly won't hurt you and will definitely help more than what you're doing now – two hundred forty hours of music, dumb talk, and redundant news about things that you have no control over, and just tend to terrorize you.

Here's another hot tip. Go to Radio Shack and spend a few dollars (probably the cost of four packs of cigarettes or six beers) and buy a hand tape recorder. Then tape your sales pitch and any other ideas that pop into your head. Then listen to yourself over and over. That's what the person you are trying to persuade is hearing. Don't you want to know what's going into their ears when you're using your friendly persuasion? This is even true for those of you young dudes and dudetes who are trying to court the opposite sex. Try your pitch on tape, listen to it, embellish it, develop it as perfect as possible before you use it again.

Who said "PRACTICE MAKES PERFECT?"

Everybody!

Here's one to think about. Planning to ask your girlfriend's father for her hand in marriage? Do guys still do that? Are you really only asking for her hand? Who's fooling whom? (Only kidding) Tape it first and listen to it. Would you say yes if it was your daughter?

Planning to ask the boss for a raise? Do you deserve one? Are you anxious about being rejected? If you don't think you deserve a raise, neither will the boss. Tape your plea and listen to it. Image the boss saying "YES."

After all this positive activity, if you ever feel you must go back to an expensive seminar again, forget about it. Pocket the money! Scratch a ticket! You're only going to hear the same material over and over again. Hey, you already have it on a CD and can listen to it at no charge.Do you really think they're going to come up with some new formula to make you a better persuader? The answer is NO! Sorry about that fact!

Did I at any time tell you that there is anything "NEW" in this book? No, I didn't! There is nothing new in "SUCCESS MOTIVATION" to learn. It's all in the last course you took and translated in this easy-to-learn book.

By the way, if you decide not to become a product or service salesperson for a living, don't be dejected. Everyone isn't cut out to be a successful product or service salesperson, or it would be a mighty crowded field. It isn't a fault to not be that type of person - just as it isn't a crime to not be a baseball player, a professional singer, movie actor, or doctor. It isn't even against the law to be an attorney.

In our free society you can attempt any field you feel passion for. Then the work begins! If the field you select is a passion – all the more power to you - and all the more fun you'll have pursuing it.

The philosophies contained in the pages of this unique sales alphabet can work for you in whatever field of endeavor you choose – especially if you choose it and don't allow it to choose you.

CHAPTER FIFTEEN

N
Now
(nou) adj.)

At the present time, immediately, at once.

When is the best time to do something?

Scarlet O'Hara said in *Gone with the Wind*, "I'll do it tomorrow. Tomorrow is another day." But, if you recall the movie, she lost.

We now know that tomorrow never comes. People who put things off until tomorrow are labeled "PROCRASTERATORS."

Here's a good line you can use: "Hey, man, I don't procrastinate anymore. Just wait, you'll see."

I like to do everything yesterday, or at least when I'm first presented with the task. That's "NOW." Do it now and it will get started sooner and get done sooner. Common sense! This is especially true of lousy tasks - the stuff that we'd rather not do at all. Why? Because if you wait, not only will it be just a difficult when you do it, but the anxiety of the anticipated outcome will grow and grow. Let's face it, the reason we are putting it off in the first place is because we really would rather not do it. It just isn't fun or we'd do it fast.

Right?

Fortunately for me I learned to never "WAIT" for permission ιο do something that I felt must get done to advance an honest project and help others.

People who put things off, even for a day, fall into that ninety percent category of sheep.

Do you want to be a sheep? Moo! No, that's what cows do. What kind of sound does a sheep make? Baa! See, I did attend college.

In this free country sheep still get three meals a day (or at least two). Ask yourself this: "When I look in the field of sheep, what do I see?"

The answer is always the same. You see a bunch of sheep and one shepherd. Which are you? Who would you like to be? What are you willing to do about it? What risks are you willing to take? Aren't you glad it is in your hands? "You are where you are because that is were you choose to be."

"Life may not be the party you hoped for, but while you're here, you might as well dance."

Would you like to be in that top ten percent of people who were put on this earth to be shepherds – a person who controls his or her own life, gives himself or herself permission to act and calls his or her own shots, writes his or her own script?

It's your choice!

In this country we are free to succeed, fail and even lose.

Listen for the music. If its not there, hum your own tune.

We really don't have to do anything we don't want to do. We can even vocalize our displeasure if we choose.

Frankly, I'd rather just plod along and plant little, positive seeds in my own garden. Maybe others will see how green my grass grows and how my flowers bloom and decide to follow suit. Teach by example!

I recall a baseball coach from my youth who told his boys, "Hustle never goes into a slump." We won a lot of games.

I recall a "Human Resource" executive who explained what he looked for from his applicants. "Attitude is seventy-five percent," he said. "I can teach the other twenty-five percent to a numb-skull. But I can't ever teach attitude."

So if you do everything "NOW" and "NEVER WAIT" you'll be way ahead of most of the rest, and it will be identified as hustle and a good attitude. Try the opposite and you'll be labeled a "SLACKER".

And remember – "NOW" spelled backwards is "WON".

I know you want to be a winner.

CHAPTER SIXTEEN

O
Obsess
(ab-ses') v.

To preoccupy the mind excessively.

This, of course, can be a negative depending on what a person is obsessed with. On the other hand, how about if you were blessed with something positive? How about if you were obsessed with your job? Wouldn't that be a neat blessing? That's why it's so important that you choose your vocation and not allow it to choose you.

EXAMPLES: One of the most successful people I have ever come in contact with develops shopping centers with zeal. He started small, built diligently, and today is one of those billionaires that "Forbes Magazine" write about - and he earned every penny.

Everyone has a hobby of some sort (or should).

I once asked my retail pal what his hobby was – what he enjoyed doing in his spare time or on his vacation. The answer was that his hobby was his work. He had passion for his chosen profession. Lucky him!

Many years ago he and his wife purchased a summer home on Nantucket Island. During his first vacation there he read for a day, beached for a day and then felt the itch to wander around.

He walked into an old First National Supermarket, found out it was for sale and bought it.

What do you think his fervor was – his obsession – his dreams – his wishes? What do you think his hobby was?

Howard Hughes had a passion. He loved flying – so one day he bought TWA. Of course, he could afford it. Before he passed away he admitted that the only thing he ever really loved was flying.

I had this other friend who loved horse racing. He attended the racetrack every day. I always went out of my way to say hello. After a few years I noticed that he didn't look quite as well dressed as I remembered. I asked him how his family was. He told me that he had lost his family.

"Your job?" I asked.

"Lost that too," he said.

So much for being obsessed with something habit forming.

Don't get the wrong message. Money isn't necessarily the measure of success in a person's life. But following your passions in a positive manner is.

If you truly want to climb into that ten percent success group of shepherds, you must be willing to become passionate (obsessed) with what you are doing. If you don't love it, it won't love you. So be very careful what venture you select, or what endeavor selects you. If you don't feel the passionate drive to spend 24/7 at it, as Tony Soprano says, "Forget aboud it."

CHAPTER SEVENTEEN

P
Preface
(pref' is) n.

To introduce by or provide with an introductory statement.

Prefacing is probably the most important art in persuasion. If we learn to preface correctly our ideas will be accepted a lot faster and easier. It is the key to creating an atmosphere in which the other person will be comfortable doing what you want them to do.

In the field of sales, a salesperson's sales can quadruple overnight. People will begin to listen and you will find that you are becoming more influential. You will also discover that you can say things to people that you might have never dared to in the past eliminating the anxiety of rejection.

How about this? "It's none of my business, but etc., etc., etc.?" It's been proven psychologically that people will not repeat your words in answering you. The person you are persuading will never say: "It's none of your damn business," after you've just prefaced your remark with, "It's none of my business, but ---." Therefore, by using this preface, you can ask just about any question that is none of your business.

Try it out on your friends and neighbors. You'll be surprised at how many intimate facts will fly out of their mouths – some of them surprisingly candid.

I'll never forget an innocent but embarrassing conversation I had on the telephone with a highly successful real estate developer's secretary when out of the blue she confessed to me that she was having a hot affair with her boss – even some blow by blows. I had never talked to her before that call. In that particular case I began to suspect that maybe my manner of selling was too influential (maybe even magical). I never used it to blackmail him like in those grade B movies on cable at three o'clock in the morning staring C. Thomas Howell, Jeff Fahey or Michael Madsen.

The greatest preface is when you know (or think you know) that you're right about something, but aren't sure that the person who you're addressing will agree. You say, "I could be wrong, but - - - etc." They may not agree, but will never say you're wrong. Why? Because you already admitted it's a possibility.

Before reprimanding or correcting someone, always preface with a compliment. That builds them up and strengthens them for your letdown. "You are doing a wonderful job in this area (pause), but I think this other area you are working on could be improved."

When I telephone a prospect I always figure that he or she is busy. Why? Because the prospect probably couldn't afford to buy my product if he or she wasn't a busy person. So I preface by suggesting that I have something that they can benefit by using and that I won't take more than a minute of their time because I know that they are busy. And I suggest that I am not really trying to sell them anything, but I am just a messenger. If the prospect is still listening I then must compact my sales pitch into about fifty seconds – or else.

By practicing my intro many times it encompasses maybe twenty seconds, and you must practice because it only comes across as sincere if you are using your words and not someone else's – words that you are comfortable with.

FACT: The important, successful boss's secretary's job (among other things) is to keep salespeople from reaching the boss. Right?

What does that mean to you?

A good salesperson "FIRST" must learn how to bypass the secretary. In order to reach the decision maker in a company you must sell the secretary. It's called "getting your foot in the door," - the phrase created many years ago by the long, lost door-to-door salesman.

Let's face it, most of us really don't like salespeople and immediately go on the defensive when we think we are being exposed to one. The salesperson who prefaces best is the salesperson who has a chance of getting through to us – then at least earning a few minutes of our valuable time to pitch their wares.

Prefacing really falls into the category of planting thoughts in the other person's mind. You can study that technique by practicing on your new palm-sized tape recorder.

Many years after my schooling days were over I enrolled in a course called Psychology 101. I mentioned it earlier as another valuable "human relation's" course that should be a prerequisite in all high schools. I advise you to buy the textbook and read it. It will teach you the value of climbing into the other person's mind. Reading Psychology 101 will teach you how to walk a mile in the other person's shoes, how to look through someone else's eyes and how repetition not only works with animals, but humans as well. You've heard of Pavlov's dog.

We also mentioned earlier that statistics show that eighty percent of all sales are made after the fifth presentation. That being true, how could any of us possibly think that we can "sell" anything after just one or two phone calls or personal presentations?

Can't be done!

I don't think a guy takes a hot chick on the first date and then proposes. It takes at least five, doesn't it?

Do you recall who always gets the grease in the adventures of the squeaky wheel?

If you could hire a hypnotist to help you get your ideas across and get people to do your bidding, would you do it?

Why not? The hypnotist certainly would know the art of "CREATING AN ATMOSPHERE IN WHICH THE TARGETS WOULD BE COMFORTABLE DOING WHAT YOU WANTED THEM TO DO."

That's what selling is all about – breaking down the defenses of the other person, building a trust, and then not abusing it. A hypnotist can do that easily by making you count backward from 100.

Have you ever seen a professional hypnotist in action? Isn't that exactly what they do?

"Bark like a dog."

"Woof, woof."

Am I right?

Learn to preface and you will be emulating a hypnotist.

Work on it tomorrow morning. Go out of your way to sincerely compliment someone. Then observe their reaction. Tell someone how good he or she is, how nice he or she looks, recall something they did that was above average – do it over and over (maybe five times), then watch. They'll eventually believe it and remember where they heard it.

"PREFACE YOURSELF." Once you take control of your own life you will no longer be relying on others to take care of you. Thus, if you wait for someone else's compliments, or pats on the head, you may never receive any morale boosting flattery. Sorry about that!

It's lonely at the top and that's where you'll be headed after using the lessons learned from the "ALPHABET TO SUCCESSFULLY SELLING YOURSELF AND IDEAS."

Start your daily dialogue with your mirror like the witch in "Snow White." "Mirror, mirror on the wall who's the fairest one of all?"

I'm not kidding. This may be the most important boost in your quest for success and erasing the anxiety of rejection. Preface your day by telling yourself how good you are over and over again in the mirror – then believe. I guarantee you will no longer be afraid of being rejected. Why? Because he who rejects you and your ideas will be the loser – not you.

I could be wrong, but: "Prefacing can be the most powerful weapon in your arsenal."

Learn to use it!

CHAPTER EIGHTEEN

Q

Questions
(kwes'chan) n.

An expression of inquiry that
invites or calls for a reply.

Questions lead to answers (replies). Your task is learning how to turn your questions into the answers you are seeking. When you're teaching yourself to be a positive force, ask as many questions of successful people as you can. Be humble, admit you don't know all the answers and you'll be surprised at how many big, knowledgeable people will take pity on you and help you. Let's face it, these people are your role models, the people you want to emulate. You'll also find that successful people have a lot in common. So remember to ask and you will receive.

When I started in business and attended a big function to network I would always eat my pride, make sure to call ahead and confess that I was a shy kind of person, didn't know anyone and ask if somebody would hold my hand and introduce me around. My request was never denied and always paid off in spades. Usually the person leading me around and introducing me was one of the more respected people in the room. Since I knew that I was educating myself on how to help others, I certainly didn't feel belittled by allowing people to help me. Boy, did I feel humble.

I try to read most of the best selling books. Why? Because it gives me a handle on what the majority of people who know how to read are thinking - whether I agree with them or not. I also try to read one biography out of every five books I tackle. Why? Biographies are written about successful people, so I learn from them, whether they are movie stars, baseball players, or presidents. They all set their sights on one goal, focus, prioritize, put everything else second, and passionately go for it. If they didn't, no one would have wasted time and energy writing the biography.

If you can't focus on one goal and are not willing to take at least the next three years out of your life and dedicate yourself towards this endeavor, you might as well quit before you start. If you are not willing to put your hand to the plow, I guarantee that you're crops will never grow. But, if you're willing to make that sacrifice, pay the price; take the risks - read on. Remember, "No pain, no gain."

I never agreed with the trick-closes that are taught in many sales courses. I mentioned earlier that I once worked for an encyclopedia company. It lasted one day. The sales pitch was written and had to be memorized. It was also filled with trick closes. Good ones, but phony.

Something wasn't right about the picture of calling on a poor family and attempting to sell them something they couldn't afford and truly could live without. Believe it or not, they were the best prospects. "Don't you want your child to be as smart as the other kids?" That was the "CLOSE." You'd be surprised how many times it worked. Why? Not many prospects said "NO" to that trick question.

It rubbed me the wrong way and I swore to never become a salesperson. I was twenty-one. What do twenty-one year olds know? Sadly, most of them think they know everything. Isn't that

Mother Nature's fault? Aren't those young people victims' to do them a big favor? Give them this book.

One of the greatest "success motivation" teachers of the day (I won't mention his name because I like and respect him and his work) has an entire chapter on trick closes - ten of them. I tell my sales people to listen to all of his CDs, but not that one.

I've discovered that if you select your prospect carefully (in other words, only address people that you sincerely believe you can help), you can use the positive approach. Ask them only "YES" questions. Tell them things that they most likely already know. Say "RIGHT?" after an obvious statement. By doing this you are creating a positive atmosphere. When you are ready to "CLOSE," don't ever ask a "yes" or "no" question like: "Do you want to buy?" or if it's your date or spouse, "Do you want to go to the movies?" Just help them "IMAGE" what it will be like after they have already bought your product, service or idea. It is up to your ability to create the "YES" atmosphere. You also know that the final result will be positive and good for them.

Sincerely believe you are doing them a good deed.

One of the greatest ways to kill a sale or a suggestion is to ask if the other person agrees with you. Why? Because it makes them think. That's a disservice to someone who is already busy. Accept the fact that you're the specialist in what you do, and they're the specialists in what they do. You aren't questioning their knowledge. You are informing them of yours. You don't ever ask if what you are suggesting can help them. Why? Because you have already determined that it can and you have given yourself permission to inform them of this fact. That's called "the power of positive thinking," and I guarantee it's infectious. If you're excited about the words exploding from your mouth, the person you are addressing will respond to that energy.

Positive energy is infectious. Unfortunately, so is negative energy - and more so. Stay as far away from negative energy as possible. If you allow it around you, it will swallow you up and all the lessons that you learned from this book will be for naught.

Whatever you want in life, image yourself already having it. In selling, image the sale already made - then create an atmosphere in which the prospect agrees with you. If you believe it strongly enough, so will the prospect. When the sale is ready to be made, you never ask questions, just give positive answers. You have given yourself permission to make the sale.

Congratulations.

CHAPTER NINETEEN

R
Reality
(re-al'I-te) n.

The quality or state of being actual or true.

This might be the "KEY" to everything in this book and in your life's trip. And, very difficult to grasp and understand. I'll try to explain. Not easy!

One of the most difficult things in life is learning to deal with reality. Of course, one cannot do that until they seek and find out what reality is. There is very little difference between "TRUTH" and "REALITY", despite the definition – the quality of being true.

Quality doesn't actually make anything true, but if enough people accept it as truth, well, sorry, it becomes "REALITY".

Everyday we are faced with reality or truth versus opinions. Opinions can be debated, truth cannot. It's a waste of time to debate the truth.

What is truth?

The sun comes up in the morning and sets at night. That is truth and not debatable. So, it is "REALITY".

Wait a minute! If it's cloudy all day the sun doesn't appear. Right? That still makes the truth that the sun comes up, but "REALITY" is that no one sees. I agree that this is pretty deep. How about in a political election, the guy who gets the most votes

- wins. That's the truth, and you can try and debate it all you want, but it becomes reality.

Wait a minute! What happens when one candidate gets the most votes, but some aren't counted and some are disqualified? What do we call that?

How about a baseball pitcher who throws a pitch that misses the outside corner and the umpire calls "STRIKE THREE"? Is that "truth"? Is that "reality"? Is that just the umpire's opinion?

So in the definition, the quality or state of being actual or true, the key is the word "QUALITY" or the word "STATE" - not the word "TRUE". What's true is true and not debatable. The umpire's opinion makes the strike true and reality. Sorry – the batter is out no matter how much he argues.

The votes in an election make the final result true. So REALITY is what things are perceived to be and are accepted as true and not necessarily always the real.

Which is more important? Unfortunately the entire key to this deep discussion is that "TRUTH" isn't always what makes the world go 'round. On the other hand "REALITY" is the more important aspect of how we should rule out lives. "REALITY" is more important than "TRUTH". Sorry!

Have I mixed you up enough?

Here's a lousy example of "REALITY" that probably affected too many people. Did the Iraqis have weapons of mass destruction? Truth says that they didn't. But "REALITY", even though it turned out to be factual, was the ruling factor and people acted on it. That is why we have to be aware of "REALITY" and sometimes respect but ditch the truth.

Sorry!

Life is like a game. It has rules.

Perhaps that's the true value of children playing sports in school - to learn competition and how to play by the rules.

If you don't follow the rules in basketball, after five failures you must leave the game.

In hockey, one failure and you spend two minutes in the penalty box.

In football, it's either five or ten yards backwards.

Thus, we learn in early life that if we don't follow the rules we will be penalized.

In other words, follow the rules or lose. And the rules are dictated by "REALITY", not necessarily "TRUTH".

When I entered the business world I soon woke up to the truth (REALITY) that the competition was keen, and those who didn't learn the rules would soon fall by the wayside just as in sports. The prisons are overcrowded with those who decided to make up their own rules and bankruptcy courts filled with those who didn't learn them well enough.

It doesn't matter how great your product is if you don't know how to promote it. That is the grim, undebatable truth. It is also true that if you have a lousy product and promote the hell out of it, you might succeed.

Sad, isn't it!

By the way, we are still wrestling on the difference between truth and reality.

I knew a man in Boston named Joseph R. Levine. Maybe you heard of him. He had an idea. Take a horrible movie and promote the hell out of it. Maybe spend a million making the flick, then five million promoting it. This was in the seventies. He bought a poorly made Italian epic called *Hercules*. He dubbed it into English, opened it in numerous theaters nationwide after saturating newspapers and TV with advertising. It worked! He made millions.

The truth is that the movie stunk. The reality is that lots of people went to see it.

I had never taken an economics course in high school or college, but soon realized that in order to stay in business for very long I had to bring in more money than went out. Simple? Common sense? But I didn't have the slightest notion on how to make that equation work. In seeking advice on whether or not to start a newspaper some sage person was kind enough to tip me off on the national averages. One in ten publications succeed and it takes any business an average of three years to turn a profit – if at all.

I also discovered that successful people make their own luck. Skill and hard work give you a fighting chance. Waiting for "Lady Luck" to wink at you is a fruitless endeavor.

A reality check showed me that people look out for themselves and always put themselves first. Too bad they never taught me that course in school.

I also detected that people like to hear themselves talk and that they like to be complimented.

I found myself in the midst of a "ME" world. Everything had to be about the other guy if I wanted to succeed. In other words, I had to put myself second. What a shock! If that was the rule (REALITY and truth), I'd have to learn to follow it.

Sales are the driving force of any business (or what you accomplish in your every day endeavors), and the "RULE" is to "create an atmosphere in which the other person is comfortable doing what you want him or her to do".

Here's something else I learned by listening. You are either in control are out of control – no in between. In order to succeed you have to always be in control. Hard work, but worth it.

In business, the client is king – he's always right. That's another rule.

That brings up Sam Walton again. He decided to make the client king in his discount stores - Wal-Mart. He bent over backwards to give service with a smile. And, it worked. Simple reality philosophy! Right? Are you still with me?

Times do change – constantly. Successful people don't fight change, but go with the flow and try and stay a step ahead.

No matter what your age, don't use it as an excuse to not stay up with the latest electronic inventions. You can now take snapshots with your cell phone and even develop the pictures in your own home. Try it! It's fun and can be learned by anyone with a little patience.

Getting back to Sam Walton, he wrote a book on giving service and how it eventually comes back ten-fold. I wonder where he learned that idea. My company also followed that rule - and it worked.

One of my first mentors used to preach that one should always jockey for position and get the upper hand in order to make a deal. I thought about that advice, watched him in action and cringed every time when I realized how uncomfortable the prospect was becoming. I decided to do just the opposite, but always wondered how many more deals that man would have completed if he had been humble instead of proud and bullish. I guess we do learn from our peers, even if it is to do the opposite.

You can learn from everyone, and it's always better to learn from someone else's mistakes (misjudgments), than your own.

I always concentrated on creating an atmosphere in which the prospects were comfortable doing what I thought was best for them. I attempted to view the situation through their eyes that built a state of sincere trust and relaxation. They were no longer defensive. They knew I was thinking about their success and welfare – and cared. Then I gave myself permission to offer the deal from what I thought was their point of view.

If you are on the side of your prospect, it becomes two against none and the majority always has the edge. That's "REALITY". Basic common sense works more times than not.

I built a bond with the client in which I would serve him and he would serve me back, without questions, or doubts, or losing any sleep. It was a nice, positive situation.

I remember one client - a little Napoleon. We've all met his type - short, spoiled, rich and pushy. He would telephone me and insist, "Hopkins, get the hell on over here. I want to see you." I wonder that if he's reading this he'd recognize himself.

Fortunately, I had learned the rules of the game. He was the most successful landlord in the city and he was asking me to jump when he spoke. Was my job to make him happy? Was my job to create an atmosphere in which he was comfortable doing what I wanted him to do? He was actually making it easy for me to do that. He was tipping his hand – telling me exactly what he wanted – what would make him happy. He wanted people to jump to his commands. Most prospects won't make it that easy for you. Most people spend weeks, months and years trying to figure out what other people want. (Have you yet figured out the wants and needs of your mate? Are you acting on it? – and if you are – isn't your relationship a lot better?)

My client was quickly revealing his wants and I was in a position to fulfill them by just a visit and biting my tongue. I had also learned that hard "FACT" that humble wins and pride loses, so I jumped, swallowed my pride, dropped everything, jogged up to his office and did his bidding.

You know what? When I needed him to do something, I respectfully telephoned him and he always answered. He didn't do that for everyone and he never turned down my bidding.

Would I have liked to have told him to "shove it?" Yeah, I guess that sometimes I would have. But what would that have gained me? A moment's macho satisfaction? It certainly wouldn't have gained me a good client and it wouldn't have made him happy.

Next time you're debating whether or not to be humble, re-member that your whole plan revolves around creating an atmo-sphere in which the other person is comfortable doing what you want him or her to do. When you reach that point, you have won the game. That's "REALITY/TRUTH". That's nature's rule.

And here's the hardest reality/truth rule of all. Ready? It isn't what is; it's what people think it is. Not fair, but true. Want to debate that? Sorry! You'd be wasting your time.

Case in point: The Salem Witch Trials. Do you think all those poor women were witches? They were hanged, tortured and burned at the stake. In other words, it wasn't what was; it was what enough people thought it was, or were coerced into think-ing it was (same difference).

"REALITY" is what people think (not know), and how they ultimately vote.

Ever wonder why Lady Justice wears a blindfold? Maybe the time has come in our society that she takes it off.

CHAPTER TWENTY

S

Strike Out
(strik' out') n.

In baseball, an out made by a batter charged with three strikes and credited to the pitcher

Successful people are willing to fall down. They know that each time they fall forward and get up; they find themselves one step closer to where they're going.

My wife, a former thoroughbred racetrack jockey and one of the first women in the country to tackle that dangerous profession, won over 1000 races and fell many times. What did she do? She got right back up and raced the next day.

When she was seven her father put her up on the back of a pony who immediately ran off with her. "Let me do that again," she pleaded excitedly.

And he did!

In golf the key is to "advance the ball." If you can do that consistently you will eventually get to the hole. I've seen people hit a golf ball that ends up behind them. Not funny if that person is you. But then you hit it again and again.

Why do people become addicted to golf? I guess it's because it resembles life. No matter how many times you play the same hole (analogous to every 24-hour day of your life), it is different.

Babe Ruth led the league in strikeouts every year, but he also reached base the most times. He was willing to fail in order to succeed.

You'll never get a hit if you're anxious about striking out.

Thomas Edison cracked a big smile when he failed for the four thousandth time in discovering how to turn on an electric light. When asked why he was happy, he replied: "I've now discovered four thousand ways that this won't work, so I can cross them out and move forward." He certainly didn't display any anxiety of rejection.

All successful people fall on their faces many times, but they also are willing to get up and keep advancing. That's where the eighty percent rule is derived from. Eighty percent of all sales are made after the fifth presentation. How many of you make only one attempt when desiring a certain outcome?

Wow! That's a lot of raised hands.

I recently attempted to reach someone who I knew was avoiding me because she owed me money. I wasn't even selling anything. I gave myself permission to place a phone call every single day until I received a callback.

Patience and persistence!

After fourteen days – oops, she picked up the phone.

Did I blast her?

No!

Did she deserve to be chastised?

Yes!

But I was pleasant, humble, and charming.

Do you think she will return my next call?

Maybe!

If she doesn't, I'll just keep on calling.

By the way, she paid me back without me even having to ask.

Many times it is that little extra step that is the difference between success and failure. It's easy to give up if you don't know where you're headed. That's why it's imperative to write down your goal, place it in plain sight and look at it 24/7. Keep chasing it and soon you will become your goal and nothing will be able to stand in your way.

Remember Thomas Stearns Eliot? "Only those who risk going too far can possibly find out how far one can go."

CHAPTER TWENTY-ONE

T

Time
(tim) n.

A nonspatial continuum in which events occur in apparently irreversible succession from the past through the present to the future.

What do they say? Time is money? Ever save coins? Stamps? Baseball cards? Ever save string? All can be accomplished to someone's pleasure. But time? It's probably the most valuable commodity in the universe, and probably the most wasted commodity. Can you save it? No! And if you could figure out the formula, you'd become the richest person in the world.

Want to hear something really scary? Most of time is an illusion. Everything in the past is memory. Everything in the future is imagination. The only thing that is completely "REAL" is this instant – the present – and that doesn't last very long and is constantly changing from imagination into memory. So you see, most of our time is an illusion and you can't save it – so you better use it as wisely as possible.

Like so many others I spend too much time thinking about the past and the future. But can we really count on even being around tomorrow?

Every day there is at least one full page in your daily newspaper devoted to people who may have spent a lot of time yesterday planning for today, only to discover the hard way that they wasted their time.

Here's a good quote from Anon: "Life is a gift from the Creator and what we do with it is our gift back to Him." (or Her if she's Mother Nature).

My father used to say, "Find it now and look for it later." It took me a little growing up before I realized what he actually meant. So I say to you: "DO IT TODAY AND PLAN IT TOMORROW." If you learn to trust your judgment you will find it easier to give yourself permission to do that. Remember what happens to those who wait for the "RIGHT" time to do something. It never comes. And also remember that if you should make a misjudgment (positive thinkers don't make mistakes, just misjudgments), and you are around tomorrow, swallow your pride and fix it then.

Here's another scary line for your diary that you don't want to get caught up in: "Life is what happens while you're making plans."

Allow me to give you a timesaving tip I learned many years ago from one of my mentors. Follow this and you'll cut your wasted time in half.

Ready?

Buy a simple 8 1/2 X 11" school notebook, lined pages. Write the month on the cover. On top of the first page write today's date. Then number the lined spaces one through whatever. Now write down what you plan to do today, one by one. As the day progresses and you receive written messages, instructions, mail, email, etc., record them in your book.

On day two write the new date on top, then bring forward all the items that weren't accomplished on day one. Also add anything you plan to do that day. At the end of the notebook, transfer what I call "IMPORTANT TELEPHONE NUMBERS" to the back of your new notebook. These are people you think you may call again at some later date. And so on a so forth.

Yes, I know, I see some of you raising your hands and wanting to tell me about a computer program that does it much better. However, I'll challenge anyone of you to beat me in finding a telephone number, or anything else contained in my little notebooks and your computer. As a matter of fact, I can probably find what I'm seeking even before your screen illuminates. And, I can easily carry my notebook with me, or read it while soaking in the bathtub.

So much for progress and computers.

PS: I'll still beat your Palm Pilot, Blackberry or Sidekick.

SAD STORY ABOUT PROGRESS: One day I walked by a salesperson's office and saw him sitting at his desk doing nothing.

"What are you doing?" I politely asked.

"Nothing," he politely responded.

"Why aren't you doing something?" I questioned, now concerned. "Are you ill?" I had discovered a long time ago that the biggest problem with doing nothing is that you never know when you're finished.

"My computer went down," he said.

"So what?" I asked, now quite irritated. I never get irritated.

"All my client information is in my computer," he said.

"All their telephone numbers are either in last week's newspaper ads, in the phone book, or with the Information operator," I said, and threw my hands in the air.

Was this clown stupid?

No!

That would have been too easy of an excuse. He was just a modern salesperson dictated by an electronic world controlled by computers and was totally lost without them.

Heaven forbid what would happen to the world if all computers decided to malfunction. You couldn't even make a bet at the racetrack – but I'd still have my scribbled notebook.

Start your notebook today and hold onto it for dear life. I guarantee it will never malfunction or need new batteries.

By the way, mention any day over the past several years and I can tell you exactly who I telephoned - and sometimes even recall why.

I sincerely believe that my antiquated notebook routine saves me time and a lot of grief.

CHAPTER TWENTY-TWO

U
Us
(us) pron.

The objective case of we.

Back in my brain-picking days I spent an informative evening with a successful equipment company owner. The more he poured down the drinks, the more he babbled about how he'd become so prosperous. I pretended to stay up with him drink-wise (many a plant died in my presence because of my generous watering them with excess alcohol). But I kept my mind awake in order to learn. Some wise tidbit might slip out of his slurring mouth.

Before the evening concluded, he looked me in the eye with his blurry ones and said, "If you ever succeed in business, don't forget to look around you and see who's standing there."

I never forgot those words of wisdom. And when I did succeed, I did look around and saw who loyally helped me over the bumps and grinds and I made sure they were well compensated for the rest of their lives.

To this day I have never discovered any successful human being who didn't need help on some level. Even in a "ME" world the final accomplishments are made by "US".

As the old cliché says, *No man is an island unto himself.*

Even Robinson Crusoe had Friday.

CHAPTER TWENTY-THREE

V

Victim
(vik' tim) n.

One who is tricked, swindled or taken advantage of.

This is probably the most difficult concept for us to accept. Why? Because human nature impels us to blame everyone and everything else for our failures – thus, the sad fact is that if we are not responsible for something that goes wrong, we can't possibly fix it. Hey, if that's true, then in makes common sense that if we are willing to bite the bullet, be humble and take responsibility for every damn thing that happens to us, then we at least have a fighting chance to fix it. But, sadly, when something goes wrong, we all instinctively look around for someone else to blame, and we become what is labeled a victim.

Guess what? People feel sorry for victims because victims can't help themselves. I feel sorry for victims for another reason - because they always lose and that isn't fair. Everyone should at least be given a chance at success in a land of plenty – the so-called land of equal opportunity.

So what is the secret?

If victims lose, how does one become not a victim? Open your ears and listen with an open mind and I'll tell you. Remember, it isn't easy! Anything worthwhile in this life isn't supposed to be easy! No pain, no gain! When you hear what I'm about to tell you, don't disagree or argue, even if you can find faults in my statements. If you do, and refuse to accept this concept, you can gladly remain a victim and a loser. But, it is your choice. I'm just giving you another choice and suggest that you seriously consider it for your own welfare and those around you who you care about, because you will become a completely different person – a positive one who begins to win.

Do you remember when you began reading this book I gave you an honest warning that if you seriously read and comprehended, it would totally change your life. Hey, I wasn't kidding!

Here it is!

About ninety percent of the population are victims - and victims lose. I don't think anyone would admit to wanting to lose. Even though it might make you feel good to be never blamed for anything, you will continue to lose and never know how to improve your lot in life.

Advertising is a good case in point. Those big agencies are paid millions to "SELL" the populace on their client's products.

How do they do it?

Simple Psychology 101.

Have you taken that course? It is a proven fact that if you say something enough times to enough people they will soon start to believe it.

If you study history you recall world leaders have used that tactic to mesmerize the populace into accepting their philosophies. One of the best (or worst) examples occurred in Germany in the thirties. Their leader would rant and rave at the top of his lungs, saying the same things over and over until the people bought it, accepted him as their savior and followed him to destruction.

The point I am making is that your brainwashed mind can work for you if you let it – especially since you are the one doing the brainwashing. It won't hurt anyone if you do it correctly. Tell yourself over and over again that you are in control of "EVERYTHING" that happens in your life. If you get socked in the jaw, tell yourself that it was because your jaw was in front of the other fellow's fist – not that it was the other person's fault (even if it was).

Many publications print a disclaimer that if a mistake is made in an ad it is not the fault of the publication. I do just the opposite. If a mistake occurs, no matter whose fault it is, I give the client a reprint. Why? Because I want to help the client. By taking the blame, it puts me in control.

What do I lose?

What do I gain?

You be the judge.

The next time you're reading the first several pages of your daily newspaper about auto accidents, drive-by shootings, rapes, muggings – check out the time that the events took place and where. Then ask yourself why the vic was there in the first place. Most fatal auto mishaps happen late at night – many after midnight. That's also when most people get slugged and mugged.

A person who has read this book and remembers "A" would "ANTICIPATE" that people who are hanging around barrooms at three in the morning might find their chins in front of the fist - or even worse.

I know what some of you are saying. "What about the holocaust or Rwanda or a person kidnapped in broad daylight?"

I'm not talking about out-of-control situations. I'm talking about you and me not copping out and looking for an excuse to fail.

The best way to take control of your own destiny and write your own script is to block out all the reasons to become a victim and then figure out a way to blame yourself for "EVERYTHING" that happens to you. Brainwash yourself. If it isn't your fault, you can never fix it and I feel sorry for you. But then on the other hand, if I'm busy fixing my stuff, I don't have a lot of time to feel sorry for and help the pseudo victims.

I feel comfortable thinking that I have some control of what isn't going to happen to me. I'm not going to get punched at midnight in Boston's Combat Zone because I'm not ever going to be there.

I'm not going to be killed Spring Skiing in the gorge at Mt. Washington because I'm not going to be there.

I'm not going to get a heart attack when my parachute doesn't open while skydiving because I'm going to take my wife's word for it that sky diving is neat and I'm never doing it. She did forty-four sky dives and each time the chute opened.

In other words, I've learned that we all can at least attempt to control our own lives, and what happens to them (or what doesn't happen to them).

Whatever price we pay for what we do is our fault. If you're not willing to pay the price, just don't buy it. Fact! Reality! No debate! Don't do the crime if you are not willing to do the time!

The "no victim" rule teaches that everything that happens to you is "YOUR FAULT" (even if it isn't).

A victim can't fix anything in his or her life because everything is someone else's fault.

Do you want to allow the outside elements to control your life? If you do, be a victim. But all victims become losers.

For many years I have had a plaque hanging on my office wall that reads, "Lord give me the strength to know what I can do something about, the strength to know what I can't do anything about and the wisdom to know the difference." I've subscribed to that philosophy and avoided many problems doing so. I think the key is the middle phrase. "Give me the strength to know what I can do nothing about."

What I am saying?

For those of you who don't understand what I'm saying, I'll repeat. "Give me the strength to know what I can do nothing about."

I'm telling you that you can do something about your own life and destiny. Work on that first. I won't waste time writing a list of things you can't do anything about, but suggest that most of them are on the front page of every newspaper every day.

Remember reading about the kids that demonstrated at Kent State on the war in Vietnam? Did their parents spend good money for them to skip class and demonstrate? I don't think so and I don't believe that Nixon pulled the troops out because those kids demonstrated, or because anyone demonstrated. Too bad they didn't know what they could do nothing about. Maybe schools should offer a course on that subject.

This is the ABC philosophy: If you sincerely believe that your actions can make a difference, then go for it. But study all the twenty-six letters first. "ANTICIPATE" the consequences, use your "BRAIN" and pick other brains, use your "COMMON SENSE", and make sure you aren't going to make any unnecessary "ENEMIES". Have "FUN" and try and follow the "GOLDEN RULE".

Am I "JUDGING" the people who demonstrated on the Kent State campus?

No, I'm not!

I'm just sorry that their priorities leaned in that direction.

Didn't they have anything better to do? Apparently not! My guess is that if you are reading this book you already realize that demonstrating is a waste of your valuable time – time you can't save and can be better used by improving your life.

Am I right?

Want to talk about "REALITY" again?

1.What can you do about wars?

2.What can you do about monopolies in big business?

3.What can you do about pharmaceutical companies inundating magazines and TV with their drugs that have worse side effects than cures?

4.What can you do about controlling what is printed on the World Wide Web – HOW TO BUILD A BOMB, CHILD PORN, ETC.

Let's face it gang, there are too many things that are out of our control. We are only little people wallowing in a big bureaucracy where things must be checked and balanced before stamped.

Very frustrating!

People wait, fiddle, deal, wheel and eventually address the subjects that may never get done. A nation containing a population of millions has to have checks and balances – but you don't. If all the national polls prove that only one out of every ten people succeed in their endeavors – what do those people have that the other nine don't have? Desire? Ambition? Patience? Persistence? A lack of anxiety from rejection? This book?

The one-in-ten honorable entrepreneurs that you seek to be and can learn to be by reading this book know what they want, give themselves permission to seek, and then do whatever it takes in a positive manner that never impedes the freedom of others to reach their goals.

Successful, goal-oriented people concentrate on their own back yard first and everything else second. They realize that if they can't straighten out their own house, how the hell can they interfere to help you straighten yours?

Next time you're hanging in a barroom or at a cocktail party, watch where you place your jaw and listen to all the victims solving the world's problems. Like they all have the inside information to formulate intellectual opinions on how we should run the country? Most of them have trouble running their own lives, but think they can tell us how to run ours.

Here's a sad thought: In a free society like ours, an uninformed individual's vote counts just as much as someone who's informed. In more direct terms, an idiot's vote is worth just as much as yours. That's truth and reality.

I figure that my time is best spent solving my own problems with one hand and lending my other hand to my neighbor. Then, if there is any time left over (or hands), I'll solve all the rest of the world's problems and then maybe I'll demonstrate with the demonstrators.

The next time things don't work out your way, take a few deep breaths, then analyze what you did wrong, and how you could have controlled the outcome. By practicing this action you will then squeeze into the small percentage of people who rule their own lives and write their own script, while all the victims are swallowed up in the quicksand of losers.

CHAPTER TWENTY-FOUR

W

Wish
(wish) n.

Something desired or longed for.

Don't wish and hope for stuff. Don't mix up wishing with imaging. People who wish don't do anything else. They wish and wait. That's for Judy Garland in the *Wizard of Oz*. In this life and on this planet, your wishes won't ever come true.

Sorry!

The poor soul who says he wishes he would succeed, or is hoping to succeed, or is trying to succeed – he's going nowhere. The person who emphatically states that he wants (not wishes) for something, images it already done, goes after it in a controlled manner – his wishes come true. His prayers are answered.

"Prayer indeed is good, but while calling on the gods a man should himself lend a hand." Hippocrates, the famous Greek physician, recognized as the father of medicine, said that back around 400 BC. Apparently only one in ten listened.

This is where the "power of positive thinking" comes into play.

Have you ever heard of telekinesis? People definitely can move objects with their minds. I attended a prayer course many years ago taught by a strange but educated woman from India. She told us a story about a bunch of starving people lost in a desert without any nourishment. She said there were about thirty of them and they decided to group-pray for food.

Within twenty-four hours a plane flew over and dropped supplies.

Go figure!

Ever hear the story about the pharos and building the pyramids in Egypt? I mentioned it earlier, but it is so amazing that it is worth visiting again. And since you only retain ten percent of what you are reading – you most likely forgot about it.

There is a school of thought that says that the Pharos sat in groups and used mind over matter to lift the stones into place. Who is around to argue? Certainly not me!

Thus, using the mind in a trained manner, you can pretty much get anything done that you set out to do. That's an amazing power that not enough of us practice using.

No more wishing! That only worked for Dorothy in Oz when she tapped her red slippers together and said, "There's no place like home," and found herself back home in Kansas.

On the other hand, come to think of it, that was mighty positive thinking on her part.

What is it that they say about making a dream come true?

Wake the hell up!

That's just what she did.

CHAPTER TWENTY-FIVE

X

Xtra

(ek'stra) adj.

More than or beyond what is usual, normal, expected or is necessary.

This is an easy one, especially for a salesperson. When your day is done (or you think that it's over at five o'clock) and you've put all your work utensils away, turned off your computer, primped, donned your coat, here's what you do. Stop, sit back down at your desk and make just one more call. By doing this you'll make 5 more calls a week, twenty a month and two hundred and forty a year. My addition says you have to make a few more sales by adopting this habit.

Just one more call.

Easy as "ABC".

I got my first radio job by taking that one extra step. I purchased a radio station directory that listed all the addresses of the radio stations in Connecticut. On one bitter, frigid February evening I was seeking auditions without making appointments. After many too many rejections, I noted that the next city that had a station was fifteen miles away.

It was snowing!

That was certainly enough excuse to call it a day.

My watch said five o'clock and I had been rebuffed at four stations already.

Dark and darker thoughts flashed though my mind. Should I go back to my warm digs and pour a soothing beer with some pals where I as hanging my hat? Or should I push forward to make one more possible audition and get rejected again? I hadn't yet heard about "GOALS" or *winning friends and influencing people*, or I wouldn't have debated with myself.

I don't remember why, but I made the extra call.

To my fortunate surprise I was told that the announcer who was on the air at the time of my visit was being fired the next day.

The station had an emergency opening.

I auditioned and was hired.

Ever heard of being in the right place at the right time?

It turned out that my uneducated decision (I hadn't yet learned about the "Strangest Secret") did them a favor. Where would they have found an emergency replacement overnight? Thanks to my visit, the show, as they say, went on.

That was the beginning of my illustrious career as a disk jockey. And let me tell you, that was probably the most fun job I ever had.

"Good morning ladies and germs. I'd call you ladies and gentlemen but you already know what you are. A funny thing happened to me on the way to the station this morning – a bum came up to me and said that he hadn't had a bite in three days. So I bit him. Ha, ha, ha! Hey, here's one you'll hum to, Frank Sinatra's latest, Strangers in my Nighty – I mean, Strangers in the Night."

Well, you get the point.

I was the morning man – went on the air at 5:30, and had to sound peppy and awake. Boy, did I drink a lot of coffee and smoke a lot of cigarettes. But the listeners liked all the corn, and the station was paying me the whopping salary of $95.00 dollars a week.

I also did a record hop every Friday night for fifteen bucks and gave away prizes at the local IGA grocery store one night a week for $5.00.

Could life be better?

No anxiety.

No pressure.

I even had a fan club.

Hey, I was a big fish in a little pond.

Someone was giving me a paycheck every week to play stupid records. What could be better than that?

Getting back to salespeople: try and avoid the pitfall that you exhaust yourself giving a great sales pitch to someone who isn't a decision-maker. I mean, you wouldn't propose to your girl or boyfriend's best friend and ask him or her to pass on the message.

I hope!

Take the time to convince whomever you reach on the phone that the service or product you are selling will benefit the boss of the company and that you don't intend to take more than a minute of the decision maker's valuable time. If you allow middleman or secretary to make your pitch, you are usually lost. They certainly won't pitch it as well as you do.

That reminds me of how many bosses you might reach before nine in the morning, which would really be doing something extra. I always made it a point to have my finger in the phone (the old days featured dial phones) before nine o'clock. I imaged that I'd be the first salesperson making a pitch to the prospect. I had discovered that in many successful companies, especially new ones, the boss is often first in the office (just as he or she is the last one to leave). If I am fortunate enough to get the boss, usually he or she is in a good mood because no one has had a chance to piss him or her off yet.

What do they say about the early bird? He gets the extra worm and probably the promotion.

What if you're not a professional salesperson? The same Xtra applies.

How many times a week do you say to yourself, "I'll do it tomorrow." Just like the barroom that advertises "FREE BEER TOMORROW". Tomorrow never comes, does it?

Several years ago, after many years of publishing my newspapers, I decided the time had come for me to vacate the premises and write books. I needed someone to take over the reins. I reviewed my options and decided to hire from within. I had some excellent and loyal staff members (still do), some with me for close to twenty years.

One stood out! Why?

She was the first one at work in the morning and the last one to leave at night.

Sounds like extra effort to me.

She got the job and today is successfully publishing her own newspaper.

Extra pays off!

Observe and you'll notice that those who make the extra effort fall into the one-in-ten category.

Ted Williams used to stay after the day games and take extra batting practice. He'd pay a groundskeeper to throw balls to him so he could hit a few more.

Did baseball's greatest hitter need extra batting practice?

Where were all those other players on his team who struggled to hit just .250?

CHAPTER TWENTY-SIX

Y

You

(yoo) pron.

Used to refer to the one being addressed.

You may enter this world surrounded by doctors and nurses and your mother and maybe even a twin or two, but you damn well exit the world alone.

When you accept reality, human nature dictates that all people put themselves first, and at best, you a distant second. Thus, what happens to you in your life can be left up to you – and it can be a lonely trip. Some famous philosopher once said, "If you can truly attest to one true friend during your lifetime, you have accomplished more than most." That may sound cynical, but probably true.

If you ask a young person how many friends they have, they will usually answer that they have many. Sadly, when we mature we realize that we have lots of acquaintances and very few friends – if any. One biblical line I remember from my religious days was, "No greater love hath a man that he would lay down his life for another."

How many people on your Christmas card list would do that for you?

After you were emancipated from your secure childhood nest, and you had to supply your own food, clothing and shelter, do you recall how lonely life became? How long did it take you to realize that you had to make your own way, select your own route and map your own destiny? Suddenly, the onus was on you – and the sooner you accepted that reality, you became in control – or out of control. You were finally in a position to fall into the ten percent (a shepherd), or in the ninety percent (sheep).

It was your choice!

Scary, wasn't it.

Just like most people, I've done my searching for the elusive answers. I even did some lay preaching and was accepted to a seminary. My teaching suggested that the Creator is passive, allows us free will to fail or succeed, live or die, be good or be bad. He doesn't step in and take over. We are not puppets on a string, and wouldn't want to be.

When I see a baseball player point to the sky after he's hit a homerun, I really wonder what he's doing. The Creator didn't hit it. The baseball player did. He should be patting himself on the back. I'm sure that the Creator is proud of one of His sons hitting a homerun, someone created in His image, but most likely He was busy watching another game, or war, or just napping. He did rest on the seventh day. At least that's what they tell us in the Bible.

I'm still waiting for a veracious person to win an academy award, get up in front of the audience and say," I just want to thank myself. I worked my ass off for this award."

A few years ago I remember that the best actress, Reese Witherspoon spent several boring minutes thanking everybody but me.

I recall the first lay sermon I gave. I was twenty-three years old, so what did I know? It was called "Faith can move mountains, but you have to use a shovel". I guess I knew more than I realized. We can hope, wish, plan, and pray that we get something done, but if we don't supply the shovel, it won't get done.

Have you noticed that?

So if you are a religious person, thank the Creator for giving you the opportunity to hit a home run, but thank yourself for hitting it. If you are not a religious person, still thank yourself.

A Creator gave you the gift of life. Your gift back to Him is what you do with it.

Who's the best friend you'll ever have? "YOU ARE!" Work hard at earning at least one more before you leave this plane of existance.

CHAPTER TWENTY-SEVEN

Z

Zealous

(zel'as) adj.

Filled or motivated by zeal, fervent.

As I stated in an earlier chapter, attitude is seventy-five percent of what you need to succeed. All the rest can be learned. That's why it's important to find something you can be passionate about before launching your career.

Choose your career - don't let it choose you, or allow anyone else to persuade you into something that sounds easy, or that its only selling point is that you will make immediate money - like working for your father-in-law. Not that your father-in-law isn't a nice fellow, but maybe you're just not cut out to be in his field. Ditto your mother-in-law, or even your own parents - no matter how much pressure they put on you.

When you find out how to take control of your life, you'll begin to choose your acquaintances, what you do, and when you do it. Whatever you choose, realize that it will take valuable time – and if you have to spend eight priceless hours a day doing some-thing, why not do it zealously – be the best at it?

If you are doing something you like, you will have fun doing it. If you have fun doing it, you will do it well. If you do it well, you will succeed and will have fun – and so on and so forth.

I recall phoning a lawyer friend late one night and saying to him, "I'm in a jam, you have to help me."

He stopped me in my tracks and said, "I don't have to help you. Remember, no one has to do anything."

After I calmed down, and he did help me, I dwelled on his reality statement – one I had never thought about before. I had always acted the way I deemed society expected me to (like everyone else). I had done many things that made me uncomfortable because I thought I had to. Think about that the next time you're being obliged into doing something you don't want to do. Are you afraid to say "NO?" What's the downside of refusing?

Start now by giving yourself permission to make your own decisions. You have to live with yourself, for better or for worse and 'till death do you part. But, maybe you can't even get rid of yourself that easily. We don't really know, do we?

When you've built your self-esteem to the level where it should be, you will then be the captain of your own ship.

If you want to measure life by the memorable moments that take your breath away, seek and find what you are zealous about.

Choose your own destiny.

There is a shoe to fit every foot.

Find yours!

I guarantee it's there – maybe hidden, but there just the same.

As William Shakespeare said in his play *AS YOU LIKE IT,* "All the world's a stage, and the men and women are just the players in it."

That means to me, that we can follow the script written for us or write our own.

Ninety percent of the people follow the easiest path and read the lines written for them.

Ten percent produce, direct, choose the actors and star in their own play – day to day. They are not anxious about being rejected.

CHAPTER TWENTY-EIGHT

TEST

What's wrong with this picture? Since when does the alphabet have twenty-seven letters?

Did you notice, or were you so engrossed in learning and zealous about your future positive attitude toward things that you missed the well-disguised mistake.

Oops – I mean misjudgment.

Do you want time to guess?

Bzz.

Too late!

How many letters are there in the alphabet? I bet half of you say twenty-seven.

Wrong!

There are only twenty-six.

What would Sherlock Holmes deduce at this juncture? He probably would say, "Elementary my Dear Watson, Mr. Hopkins used one of the letters twice. Any clues to why he did that? Ah, ah. It is the "I". It is used twice."

Dr. Watson would probably counter with, "But he figured that one needs two eyes to see clearly." Get it? Two I's? Two eyes?

Case rests!

Do you see how a one-in-ten person has to think on their feet, and have an answer for everything?

If you buy that excuse for the two I's, I have a long bridge in Brooklyn that I'll sell to you real cheap.

The simple truth is that I made a misjudgment and included the letter "I" twice, then was too lazy to change it. But, I fooled Holmes and Watson – and maybe even you.

Here's another misjudgment I made that maybe you noticed. "H" and "L" are the same definitions: "HEARING" and "LISTENING".

On the other hand, the way I learned was by listening, so maybe my misjudgment was deliberate.

I'll never tell!

CHAPTER TWENTY-NINE

NUMBERS

Now that you have learned the *ALPHABET TO SUCCESSFULLY SELLING YOURSELF AND IDEAS,* let's do something else easy – something that you learned in grade school.

Numbers!

Maybe a dozen?

Aren't things supposed to be cheaper by the dozen?

1–12. Learn these and you'll never fail.

1

Sad but true, you only get one chance to make a first impression, so you better make sure it's a good one. That's probably why you dressed up so cool when you had your first date. Remember? You hadn't read any success motivation books at that age, but common sense and instinct told you the right thing to do.

I wonder why.

The same is true today.

Subconsciously people will always recall the first thing they heard about you, or the first time they saw you. So it had better be good. It may not be fair, but it's true (REALITY), and I hope no one ever told you life was going to fair.

Did they?

2

After a long argument, someone once convinced me that no one could ever win that type of battle, thus don't waste your time. Why? Even when you're right and you win, the antagonist will be mad at you for being right, and proving them wrong. What did you gain? You gained someone's resentment – so you lose.

I could be wrong, but the following is a truth, not an opinion, anything debatable, or anything to argue about. There are at least two sides to every story. Common sense again?

SUGGESTION: When you hear something about a neighbor, or someone in your office, client, or friend, always seek at least another side of the story before responding.

I guarantee there is one.

You'll usually be surprised at how different someone else looks at the same picture.

A sage once said, "Knowledge is power, ignorance is bliss." I believe about ninety percent of us are blissfully ignorant.

Lawyers always do their homework before going into court so they won't get any surprises. Their power comes from their knowledge of not just their client's point of view, but, even more crucial, their opponent's point of view. That adds up to at least two points of view. Don't forget that fact, and don't act until you've searched for and found at least one more point of view.

A respected friend recently described another friend as being "IMPETUOUS". I like friend number two, know she has some problems and would like to help her. I mean, isn't that why we have the second hand? So I immediately looked up the word "IMPETUOUS" in the dictionary.

Here's what it said: IMPETUOUS: Acting on the spur of the moment without considering the consequences – rash, hasty, unthinking, done without thought as a reaction to an emotion or impulse.

When I read this I suddenly felt pity for friend #2. I was sure that if I accused her of being that definition, she would act "IMPETUOUSLY".

It sounded like a lose-lose situation.

Sad!

If I could get her to read just this part of the book, maybe she would stifle herself, stop, look and listen. Isn't that what's still written on rural signs as you approach a train track.

"IMPETUOUS" people get killed on train tracks.

Stay tuned!

Making decisions on false facts can ruin you, lead to wars, and create lots of hurt feelings.

Want power?

Get some knowledge!

<u>3</u>

Three's company and 3's a crowd. You'll discover that a meeting of one (you) usually can get things done a lot faster and smoother – and if you should happen to fail at something, you'll only blame yourself. Before meeting with others, if you've been appointed the ultimate decision maker, make sure you've done all your home-work, and figure how you want it to come out – then lead it in that direction.

No surprises!

An honorable and caring dictator or an honorable and caring king is the greatest leader because he doesn't have to contend with all the bureaucracy (red tape) that keeps most governments from ever getting anything done. The king or dictator has no lobbyists to deal with. No checks and balances!

Of course, the worst government is a bad dictator or bad king. No checks and balances!

Your self-esteem now enforces the fact that you can make your own decisions, act on them, not wait for permission, and go forward. Advance the ball to your goal. If you make a misjudgment, acknowledge it, get back up on the horse and move forward.

In the movies doesn't "GOOD" always win?

Don't forget - this is your movie – you are the three important moviemakers – the director, the writer and the star.

The story plot and ending is up you.

4

Four can stand for "FORGIVE".

The greatest philosophy you can ever live by is to "GIVE, FORGIVE AND LIVE". You can't practice that enough. If you accept the reality that you must focus and give your goals one hundred percent effort to have a chance at success, where the hell will you find time to be vengeful or angry with anyone - even if you feel they deserve it?

Did you ever realize that if you hate someone it only hurts you?

It doesn't hurt them.

This is an undebatable truth and makes it a wasted emotion. Save those emotions for memorable, good stuff - and tonight say a prayer for everyone you don't like. They probably need it.

5

Five equals the fingers on your hand. We were born with two hands. Ever wonder why? I'll tell you. One is to help yourself, and the second is to help others. (I think I mentioned that one before.)

Are you in a position to help others?

The more successful you become, the more you will be in that position. Someone who "CAN'T" feed himself or herself won't be able to feed anyone else.

Have fun looking up the word "CAN'T" in your dictionary. It just isn't there.

I told you the story about when some success motivation guy conned me into purchasing a sales course on 33 1/3 RPM plastic records. Along with the course he threw in a record entitled "I CAN'T". The theme of the lecture was that there is no such thing as "CAN'T".

After listening, I totally accepted the concept. It helped me change my approach to every facet of life, especially sales. I even started correcting other people who used the word. "Look it up in the dictionary," I'd say (and still do). "The word doesn't exist."

I'll never forget calling on a major bank president to raise some badly needed funds to print my next newspaper (that was in my first year of business). He studied my P & L and finally announced, "I can't lend you any money. You're a deficit corporation." I'd never heard that word, but it sounded contrary.

I conjured up all my boldness and said, "I didn't come in here to waste your time, or find out why you "CAN'T" help me, sir. I already knew that you couldn't lend me any money. I came here to find out how you can help me."

That stopped him for a while.

He pondered my remark, smiled, picked up my little, 16-page newspaper and studied it, gave me a few publishing tips that I eventually followed, and said, "Go visit my son-in-law. He runs a second mortgage company that grants small business loans at high interest rates. Maybe he can help you."

If I hadn't learned that the word "CAN'T" doesn't exist, I'm sure that my anxiety of rejection would have stopped me when he told me "NO".

Many times since that day I have heard myself saying, "I don't want to hear how something can't be done. Tell me how it can be done."

By the way, I secured the loan and it saved my company.

I wonder where that money really came from.

666

That's the symbol of the Devil and you don't want him messing with your drive to the top.

Here are six traps he'll set for you to watch out for.

1. Don't ever put down a neighbor or competitor. Why? Because you may be insulting the intelligence of another neighbor or prospect. And don't ever bad-mouth someone's relative. Even if they can't stand the person, they will take it personally. You never know the relationship anyone has with anyone else. A sales prospect may even be using the competitor's product because he or she, in his or her wisdom may have decided to do business with them. So, watch out! Hold your tongue! I usually compliment my competitors, and then suggest why I'm a more beneficial buy.

Try it!

2. Don't ever believe in your own press clippings. Has anyone ever accused you of allowing your head to get too big for your hat? As you succeed you will begin to be proud of yourself (and rightfully so), and others will begin to take notice. Remember your humble beginnings. You will always be you. The best compliment I ever received was given me by a golf-club-champion when he said, "You know, you're the most down-to-earth-person I've ever met. I notice that you fraternize equally with everyone - rich, poor, young, old, important and dull."

Why do I find it easy to be that way? Because I always figured that if you strip everyone of their skin, then we would all look the same – a gross thought, but true. I do seek the good in others. The bad pops up real fast – the good sometimes is hidden – but there.

3. Don't ever wait until the RIGHT time to do anything you think is important. Why? Because the RIGHT time never comes. Follow your gut feelings. Your self-esteem will tell you that it is right for you to do something, and the time is "NOW". If you wait for permission, it will always be too late, or you'll never do it. The sooner you start out on a journey, the sooner you'll get there. The "RIGHT" time will never come, It never does! And, don't forget that all roads are cluttered with bumps, sharp turns, and debris. Be ready! Take them as they come, one by one. Don't let them pile up, or you won't be able to pass.

4. Remember the story about the tortoise and the hare? Those children tales all have good principles to them. The tortoise moved along slow and steady with patience and persistence. In the end, he won. Read the story again. He wins every time and so will you if you follow his lead. Patience and persistence always wins in the long run. Don't cut corners – go straight to the finish line wearing blinkers. Nothing can sidetrack you.

5. How about the children's story of the *LITTLE ENGINE THAT COULD?* Remember that one? We used to have Christmas-grabs every year at our office. One year I drew the name of my editor who was a horrible, negative thinker, constantly telling everyone why things couldn't be done. I don't allow anything negative in my office. So, I bought him a copy of "THE LITTLE ENGINE THAT COULD" and told him to read it. If you recall,

The Little Engine is trying to climb up a hill and he says over and over, "I know I can, I know I can, I know I can."

Can you?

I really don't know if my editor ever read the book, but he's seventy-nine years old now and still employed by my company.

I knew he could!

6. Eat your pride. Remember: "HUMBLE WINS, PRIDE LOSES." If you make a misjudgment, catch it fast, stop it and move on. Don't be afraid to admit that you're wrong. Better people than you and I have been wrong, and you'll be wrong many times before you're done. I don't care how smart you are or how smart you think you are; you'll stumble and make misjudgments. Remember that you are the pilot of your own plane, so recognize the errors quickly. The formula to success is to be right more times than you're wrong. But, if you're wrong and won't admit it (being in denial), you'll crash.

Z

Speaking of the Devil, ever hear of the "SEVEN DEVILS?" We all know the "TEN COMMANDMENTS" and how impossible they are to keep. As a matter of fact, they're quite outdated, since one of them demands you not covet your neighbor's ass. In Biblical days every neighbor owned a donkey, and that's what that commandment referred to. (I hope)

But, maybe we can deal with the "SEVEN DEVILS", sometimes referred to as "THE SEVEN DEADLY SINS".

Here they are:

1. Avaraice – greed.
2. Hate – wasted emotion.
3. Self indulgence – addictions.

4. Kindred selfishness – love yourself too much.

5. Hopelessness – negative thinking

6. Blasphemy (I don't know what this means, damnit)

7. Pride

Work on these and your life will be much happier – except when you drop a hammer on your toe, or miss a close putt in golf. "#%@#*&#"

The SEVEN DEVILS can be overcome - and you'll be the winner, and be happier. I guarantee.

The "TEN COMMANDMENTS"? I don't think anyone is expected to follow all of them. In my humble opinion they were written by mere men who did it politically to scare the populace and keep them in line.

8

Eight rhymes with mate.

You know the cliché that behind every great man is a woman? If that were true, wouldn't it also follow that behind every loser man there is a woman?

In a world where women now hold responsible jobs, wouldn't it follow that behind every successful woman there is a man?

At what age do we all begin seeking our soul mates? Teenagers? And how do we recognize our soul mate? Gut feelings? Is there one mate for each person? Was man created to be monogamous? Did you know that penguins stay with the same mate for life? Maybe that's because all penguins look alike.

Fifty percent of all marriages end in divorce. What does that say about human monogamy? Maybe we were all intended to have a mate to share our ups and downs, successes and failures. Someone to accompany us down the path of life. Maybe not! It is more fun to share stuff. Isn't it?

Do married people live longer?

Yes!

Why?

I guess the answer is that we were intended to mate once, twice or more.

In some societies it is acceptable to have more than one mate. How does that work?

I guess the idea of mating is viable in all species and should be worked on just a bit more than the average person you and I know. Did you ever wonder that if you spent as much time and energy on your marriage as you did on your job that your marriage might be more successful? Or - the other way around? If you spent as little time on your business as you do on your marriage - - -?

What do you think?

The quest for the right mate is probably worth the effort, and while the imaging is fun, falling in love is the greatest natural high ever created. That lasting goal is almost impossible to reach for at least fifty percent of us.

I strongly suggest that by following the "ABCs" you've learned in this book, it will raise your chances of finding your soul mate at least ten-fold.

9

Nine innings. Nine players. Baseball has always been my favorite sport. I know it's slow and tedious, that the season lasts forever and the games play too long. Maybe for some males it's an identification, or replacement.

All of the guys who played some type of baseball as a youngster, even if it was stickball or softball, raise your hand.

Hey, that's a lot. So I guess I'm right. We all had a distant dream of hitting a home run with the bases loaded and we now sit and watch Barry Bonds, Manny Rameriz or A-Rod do it over and over, feeling our bodies rise in the chair every time.

Could that be us out there? In our dreams it can.

What else is there about baseball that attracts our attention? The announcers are constantly talking about the chemistry and teamwork. Nine players take the field and work together as one in order to vanquish nine other players who take a wooden weapon to the plate and try and slash the ball through or over their enemy.

Baseball is also an escape from reality, which we all need from time to time. Your job is serious and your pleasure is supposed to be fun and relaxing. Even though your baseball team loses again and again, does it really make any difference in your scheme of life? No! Not a hill of beans difference. Maybe that's why it's so intoxicating to watch.

I suggest that we all start out the day avoiding the front page of the newspaper and CNN on the tube. Why? Because they're filled with negative energy.

Start you day by watching cartoons, an old movie and the Discovery or History channel. Read the sports page, memorize the batting averages, look at the funny page, and then finish with Dear Abby. Nothing there to ruin your day.

Sports succeed on teamwork and so will you.

Surround yourself with a good team. They don't have to be smarter than you, or better looking than you. They don't have to be fatter, thinner, louder, or even funnier. They just have to work with you as a team. If you like them, they'll like you back. Respect them, their good points and bad and they'll return the gesture.

If you equate life with baseball, then you'll be glad that it's long, active, interesting, surprising, rewarding and competitive. Competition keeps you awake, forces you to keep your eye on the ball. Whether you are in spring training, the first inning, or the

World Series, you can always hope and plan for extra innings. If you play as a team, you're guaranteed to win the pennant every year.

Go for it!

Remember: "Hustle never goes into a slump."

10

Did you ever see the Hitchcock movie *THE TEN LITTLE INDIANS?* Classic story! Mr. U.N. Owen (later revealed as Mr. Unknown) sends invitations to ten people to visit his island home. Of course, they all show up, or the story would end there.

One by one they're murdered, until only two people are left alone. Well, one must be the murderer.

Right?

Wrong!

Sometimes things aren't what they obviously seem.

Ever hear this line? "If it seems too good to be true, it probably isn't true." Be in control by doing your own checking. Then, if you are conned (I've been conned more than once), blame only yourself and feel sorry for the grifter. Under other circumstances, he could be you.

Remember, knowledge is power. Do your homework before you take the test.

I know that this philosophy contradicts an earlier suggestion that, "Life is what happens when people are making plans." Or, "Find it now and look for it later." But, what I am saying is that after reading this book you will have the mental resources, drive, desire and self-confidence to acquire the knowledge to go forward with vigor.

11

Ever shoot craps? Seven or eleven and you're a winner. Is that lucky? I don't believe in luck and neither should you. Winners make their own luck.

Wade Boggs, a former American League batting champion and now a Hall of Famer used to say, "The more I practice, the luckier I get."

You can play all the lotteries you want, but your chances of getting lucky are quite slim.

I don't knock gambling. It's fun - an escape from reality, and sometimes you can win a few dollars. "Jimmy the Greek" used to say, "You never know when your lucky day is here unless you gamble every day." I guess he was right if you believe in luck. And, if you gamble every day, a few of those days you'll win – just like the Indians who dance until it rains. They can't lose – but get mighty damp.

The difference between success and failure is a thin line, but luck doesn't come into the equation. If you make more right calls than wrong, even if it is as close as ten to nine, you'll most certainly succeed.

Of course, the opposite will result in failure.

I assure you that you can count on making more right decisions as you practice. As of now, you have learned how to make more right calls than misjudgments, and lots of memorable moments are in front of you.

Save your dice for board games.

12

Psychology Today magazine once printed the twelve most persuasive words. I wrote them down, posted on my wall and in all the sales offices, and have used them ever since.One of my salespeople actually experimented and included all twelve of them in one letter. It was kind of corny, but not bad. He now runs his own successful newspaper. Guess he used them wisely.

Here are the twelve words. You'll understand why they're the most persuasive and used in much of the national advertising we're all bombarded with. I suggest you print them out and post them – and use at least one or two of them in every letter or email you send out.

Save

Results

Easy

Guarantee

Proven

Discover

Safely

You

Money

New

Love

Health

CHAPTER TWENTY-NINE

MY MENTORS

Every successful person admits to having a mentor or mentors. I was fortunate to have one that worked beside me every day and a few others that I could communicate with through books, tapes and records.

Here, you can meet them.

Earl Nightingale (1921 – 1989)

Earl Nightingale said: "People are where they are because that is where they choose to be."

If you can believe that, then you better stop wanting to be and start being where you want to be real soon - starting by following the "ABCs" of this book.

Earl experienced a tough childhood, his father deserting the family when Earl was twelve. His mother worked for the WPA and they resided in Tent City in Long Beach, California during the horrible Depression years. I think we could all agree that Earl was not brought up with a silver spoon in his mouth, or probably sometimes no spoon at all.

As a youngster Earl spent many hours in the local library seeking the answers, especially the key to success – a literary search that would stretch over the next 20 years and lead him to study the world's great religions, philosophy and psychology. In 1941, aboard the battleship Arizona at Pearl Harbor, Earl was one of the few survivors when the Japanese attacked.

After the war Earl began a successful career in radio, eventually producing his own daily commentary on success motivation. He had discovered that salespeople far out earned the other employees.

In 1957 at the age of 35, he retired. During this time he purchased an insurance company, trained the sales force and drove the company to the top. The company's sales manager convinced him to put his sales ideas on record and it ended up as a five-minute daily broadcast that became the longest running and most widely syndicated radio show in the nation.

At age twenty-nine Earl woke up to the fact that he had been reading these same words over and over again from all his mentors: the New Testament, Buddha, Lao Tse, Emerson – just to name a few. In one form or another they all preached the same messages: "We become what we think about." "As ye sow, so shall we reap."

It is from this enlightenment that Earl wrote his *THE STRANGEST SECRET* message. He titled it that because of the irony of it all – that this truth of why we become whatever it is we become is not a secret at all and therefore it is very strange that we don't all know about it.

This disc went on to earn a Gold record, usually reserved for pop hits - the only recording if its kind to ever receive that lauded status.

Earl died in 1989.

Today he is remembered as perhaps the greatest motivation philosopher of his time.

In 1987 I had the rare opportunity to see him in person. Nothing could stand in my way. I was going to finally meet the individual who had changed my entire life. I was going to be in the same room with him and hear his forceful and inspirational words.

Hot damn!

I couldn't wait!

He was appearing at a speaking engagement in Boston, less than 35 miles from my office. I purchased a few tickets, and on the morning of the event I performed some consulting work with a young man who was just getting started in the business world. During the discussion I kept staring at the last ticket on my desk. I had always attempted to follow the philosophy of giving, forgiving and living. One major giving philosophy is to give away something that the other person wants and that you also want. It's too easy to give away old golf clubs, or clothes that don't fit anymore. So I reluctantly gifted the young chap my only ticket.

He attended the seminar and Earl announced from the stage that the audience was witnessing his last public appearance.

Less than two years later Earl Nightingale traveled to that big success motivation seminar in the sky.

He must have known that night.

My young friend immediately became success motivated and today is one of the leading commercial real estate salespeople in a top Boston company.

I have to include one more Earl Nightingale story.

In the early sixties when I was still struggling to keep my company afloat, it came to my attention that the brother of a former girlfriend had attempted suicide. I had remembered him as a leader in his school activates, a fine athlete, president of his class and eventually a member of the SOS (today's CIA). I instantly phoned him and asked if he could help me do some editorial work – maybe twenty hours a week. That was all I could afford and I figured his pride might block him from allowing me to help him. I included one catch. I insisted that he listen to *THE STRANGEST SECRET*. He agreed, and later admitted to lending his ears to it over a hundred times.

Three months later he was hired by a top stock brokerage firm (his passion).

Six months later I attended his wedding to his childhood sweetheart.

At last count he's still married to the same lady, successful in the market and playing a pretty good golf game.

Nice ending to what could have been a sad story.

I guess my friend learned how to eliminate the anxiety of rejection.

Thanks Earl!

Dale Carnegie (1888-1955)

Dale Carnegie said: "Handle complaints, avoid arguments, keep your human contacts smooth and pleasant."

I gave Dale's book to all of my children (4) when they were teens, hoping some of it would rub off on them as they matured.

It worked on the ones who read it.

In my opinion, the nicest gifts you can give to someone is your time, *THE STRANGEST SECRET CD*, Dale Carnegie's book, *HOW TO WIN FRIENDS AND INFLUENCE PEOPLE*, Norman Vincent Peale's book, *THE POWER OF POSITIVE THINKING* and this book.

If you should have a hot tip on tomorrow's race a a local horse race track, I'm sure that would be equally appreciated.

Dale, born in Missouri, was a pioneer in public speaking and personality development. He became famous by showing others how to become successful. His book *How to Win Friends and Influence People* (1936) has sold more than ten million copies, has been translated into many languages and still sells briskly every day.

Two of his most famous maxims are, "Believe that you will succeed, and, "Learn to love, respect and enjoy other people".

Dale attended a state teachers college and became a salesman for Armour and Company. In 1912 he taught public speaking to businessmen. In doing this he learned that what was most needed was training the fine art of getting along with other people in everyday business and social contacts.

Dealing with people was the biggest problem his students were confronted with. He discovered that about fifteen percent of financial success came from technical knowledge of your product or service, and the other eighty-five percent came from your skill in handling people.

He checked colleges and secondary schools seeking a course to teach this most important prerequisite.

He came up empty and he would find the same dilemma if he checked today.

He conducted a survey and health was the number one personnel interest.

Guess what was number two.

Right!

How to get people to like you!

Dale observed that people like people who like them (common sense), and that the key to handling other people is to show a sincere interest in them. Like them first and they will like you next. Sort of sowing first and reaping second.

I wonder where he learned that.

Frustrated in his search, he found no book on the subject - so he wrote one. It sold for a dime and was published at the height of the "Great Depression".

Was that the right time? My guess is that intelligent advisors would have said "NO!" But Carnegie wasn't about to be a victim, so he gave himself permission to publish it anyway.

TIP ON READING CARNEGIE'S BOOK: It's not a novel with a plot; so don't read it beginning to end. On first perusal, underline the ideas that grab you.

Keep it at your bedside.

Refer to it often.

Dale Carnegie schools still abound all over the world, and in my opinion the course should be taught at every high school here and abroad.

Bob Lewis (1921 – 2001)

Bob Lewis said, "Everyone wants a bargain, so give them what they want before they even ask. Always analyze what's the most you can give a client, friend, or neighbor for the least return to you- then do it,"

Robert O. Lewis was born in Nutley, New Jersey, served in the U.S Army and bankrupted two of his own companies (one a newspaper) before our paths crossed.

He never wrote a book or recorded a disc, but he could have. He was one of those blessed individuals who was born with a talent like Bobby Orr in hockey, Michael Jordan in basketball, Tiger Woods in golf or Ted Williams in baseball. Any of those superstars would readily admit that it wasn't all practice that made them great. Just like Beethoven wrote his first symphony at age four. Was it because of all the little guy's studying and practice? I don't think so.

Lewis ambled into my Boston office the same week I published my first newspaper. (Coincidence?)

He was a family man, forty-one years old, out of work, broke, and the bank was about to foreclose on his house.

"I'm looking for a job," he said. "A good salesman can sell anything."

I called his bluff, clipped a quarter page ad out of the Boston Globe that had nothing to do with the subject of my newspaper and handed it to him. "Sell this and you've got a job," I challenged.

Twenty-five years later he retired from my firm with a nice pension, a gold watch and moved to Florida. (I really don't remember giving him the gold watch).

Without his guidance you wouldn't be reading this book, and I wouldn't be qualified to write it.

While Lewis had never read Carnegie or listened to Nightingale, he seemed to possess all their qualities. He taught me that the client is king and even when wrong, the customer is always right.

He educated me to always give a deal.

He showed me that the small advertisers were more important than the big ones. "It takes a lot of bricks to build a big, strong wall," he said. "Did you ever notice that all the bricks are the same size and small but the wall big?"

He told me about an ad agency that survived on one enormous client with a multi-million-dollar ad budget. They had no time or patience to help the little guys. The greedy firm eventually lost the big client and went bankrupt.

Before working for me Lewis sold bowling score sheets. He showed me how they laid out the equal size blocks on top of the scorecard, then sold the spaces to local advertisers, one by one. When the sheet was full, they'd leave that town 'till the next year. They would do this in numerous towns.

Why wouldn't and couldn't the same format work in a newspaper, he wondered?

Thanks to Lewis and bowling score sheets, we tried it, and it worked. We laid out the spaces on the pages, and then filled them.

"Running a newspaper is like filling an apartment building," he said. "You build the building and then fill the spaces with tenants – not the other way around."

My newspaper was always laid out in the beginning of the week showing the empty spaces and they were all filled by the end of the week, not at all like other newspapers that allowed the sales to dictate the size.

Lewis never left a hole vacant, just like in the old days he never left a town 'till all the ads had been sold on the bowling score sheet.

He told me that you could sell an ad on anything that people look at (newspapers, magazines, TV, billboards, skywriting) and especially if it has a captive audience.

I came up with the novel idea of selling ads on a roll of toilet paper. That's certainly a captive audience and people sitting there are always looking for something to read. Right? I was serious, but we never did it.

Hey, someone could still do that and succeed.

Lewis never uttered an angry word and he never put anyone down. "If you say something against a person, whether they deserve it or not, you never know who will be injured by the remark and it may come back and land in your lap. In other words, if you can't say something nice about someone, shut the hell up."

He always spent a few more dollars than he made, so was constantly in debt. No matter how much I paid him, he was still in debt. That was good for me because he had to sell extra ads to make the extra money. (*What makes Sammy run?*)

In his mind, the sale began when the prospect said no. It was a challenge to him and he usually won.

He was the best salesperson I ever met and he taught me well.

You know how cowboys in the movies say that they want to die with their boots on? Lewis came back to work for me twelve years after he retired to help sell ads on my Internet site.

He sold three on the day of his death.

I guess for a salesperson, that's like dying with your boots on.

Jesus of Nazareth {1 AD - 33 AD?}

Jesus said: "Thou shalt love the Lord the God with all thy heart, thy soul and thy body, and thy neighbor as thyself." All the rest of the Bible is nothing but an explanation of that one sentence.

I don't think you have to be a Christian to study the life of Jesus. He has been proven to be a historic figure and whether he is "The Son of God", or not, to me is irrelevant in the everyday (on Earth) scheme of things. I'm more interested in his teachings, just as I've studied the teachings of great religious leaders – Buddha, Confucius, Muhammad, Nicon (Russian), Mary Baker Eddy and others.

When I was an inquisitive teenager I made it a point to visit every church at least once. I almost fainted from the incense fumes in the Greek Orthodox Church, but I did learn that there were many schools of thought (not too different) that swayed people's thinking.

It was an interesting study that is available to anyone who is curious.

John Grishem did the same thing in his best selling book, "THE LAST JUROR". I doubt any church would slam the door on a person wanting to attend a service. But don't forget to put a little something in the plate, and don't make change. In this life you get nothing for nothing.

My self-studies taught me that most of the religions preached a form of the *Golden Rule* - "DO UNTO OTHERS", etc.

It's too bad that there are so many religions much alike and teaching basically the same morals and can't solidify.

While Jesus of Nazareth only preached for three years, he must have been an excellent salesperson to have influenced so many. Very few of his actual words are quoted in the Bible, or anyplace else. But it is that very philosophy that I have always found quite insightful and true, and pops up in all the other success motivation books and courses.

Here's something I found buried in a bunch of old documents that may explain to some people about his long-lasting popularity.

ONE SOLITARY LIFE

He was born in an obscure village, the child of a peasant woman. He grew up in still another village where he worked in a carpenter shop until he was thirty. Then, for three years, he was an itinerant preacher. He never wrote a book. He never held an office. He didn't go to college. He never visited a big city. Her never traveled two hundred miles from the place he was born. He did none of the things one usually associates with greatness. He had no credentials but himself. He was only thirty-three when the tide of public opinion turned against him. His friends ran away. He was turned over to his enemies and went through the mockery of a trial. He was nailed to a cross between two thieves. While he was dying, his executioners gambled for his clothing, the only property he had on earth. When he was dead, he was laid in a borrowed grave through the pity of a friend.

Twenty centuries have come and gone and today he is a central figure of the human race, a leader of mankind's progress.

All the armies that ever marched, all the navies that ever sailed, all the parliaments that ever sat, all the kings that ever reigned put together have not affected the life of man on earth as much as that one solitary life.

Probably the greatest philosophy book ever written is the Holy Bible. If you eliminate all references to religion you are then left with every possible rule of life. Unfortunately, religion scares a lot of people so they stay away from that little black book.

Many years ago I was told by several business people that a person couldn't run a successful operation following The Golden Rule. "Treat others like you would like them to treat you."

I think I took it as a challenge - thus modeled my business after that philosophy, and it has always worked for me – actually getting me through three recessions.

Apparently, that's what guides people successfully through the hard times – working together and trusting. If you follow that code every day you will find it comes easy, and it's there when you need it.

How many times have you heard that if you sow first, you'll most certainly reap second - and not the other way around?

Maybe the Bible was the first success motivation book ever written and Jesus the first success motivation teacher.

And he charged nothing for his lectures.

Norman Vincent Peale (1898 – 1993)

Dr. Norman Vincent Peale said, "Believe in yourself. Have faith in your own abilities. Without a humble but reasonable confidence in your own powers you cannot become successful or happy. But with sound self-confidence you can succeed."

Born in a rural Ohio town, Dr. Peale grew up helping to support his family by delivering newspapers, working in a grocery store and selling pots and pans door to door.

For half a century he was one of the most influential Protestant clergymen in the country. He had a keen understanding of human psychology. (Do you think he passed Psychology 101?) He wrote over forty books, translated into forty languages and selling over fifteen million worldwide. He lived actively to the ripe age of ninety-five.

When I was eighteen and graduating from high school, one of my classmates was John Peale. His father, Dr. Norman Vincent Peale addressed our graduating class of over two hundred eager-to-get-the-hell-out-of-there boys. The preacher assessed the room, and it didn't take him long to climb into our heads. He related to the Brooklyn Dodgers baseball team all the positive thinking points he wanted to make. That grabbed our attention fast enough.

"Science had proved that you can only carry one thought in your mind at a time – so you might as well make it a positive one," he said.

That made sense to me and I have gone out of my way to avoid negative people ever since.

"A baseball player can stand at the plate thinking he's going to get a hit, or think he's going to strike out. It takes the same brain space and the same energy of thought," he preached. That also made sense to me and I applied the same attitude to everything I undertook. I could succeed or fail.

I opted to think about succeeding.

Many in that graduating class recently gathered to celebrate their fiftieth. I was surprised (but shouldn't have been) at the percentage of successes – maybe eighty-five percent.

Could Dr. Peale's influence have had anything to do with it?

My 26 Year Old Son's Mentor
Russell Simmons (1957 -)

I have a twenty-six year old son, Stephen, who is just entering the business world. Did you ever receive a lecture from your own son? It isn't comfortable. "Why don't you write down all your philosophies?" he bugged me over and over.

So, in order to get him off my case, I finally got off my butt and wrote this book.

I figure that we can learn by other's misjudgments, or our own. Our choice!

It seems to me that it takes longer to learn from our own. Thus, from his early teens I availed my son to all of my literature mentors, hoping some of the success motivation ideas would rub off on him. I know that Larry, Moe and Curly did rub off on him.

Recently, I noticed that he was becoming quite optimistic about everything.

He began lecturing me; *"You need to have vision before you start any venture. You're judged by the people you hang around with. Always keep an open mind to learn new things. Use patience and persistence."*

I started patting myself on the back for all the good advice I had passed onto my son.

Before my third pat he asked if I had ever heard of Russell Simmons?

I flashed an incredulous glance and then quickly confessed that Simmons wasn't on my guest list and neither was Brittany.

Russell is a multi-billionaire rap entrepreneur, the CEO of Def Jam, a vastly successful record company, is also a movie producer (The Nutty Professor) and owner of a popular clothing company (Phat Farm).

In my opinion any self-made success has an interesting story, especially if he's following the three IVE's. "GIVE, FORGIVE and LIVE". Russell Simmons says, **"People aren't good or bad, just smart or stupid."**

In my studies I have discovered that all the success motivators say basically the same things, just in different disguises.

Simmons wrote a book entitled, **LIFE AND DEF, Sex, Drugs, Money and God, Crown Publishing, a div. of Random House, Inc**. Read it and you'll see what the youth of the nation is thinking about. You'll also get the same success motivation tips Confucius and Socrates preached over 2500 years ago.

Simmons talks about becoming successful by surrounding yourself with good people and respecting and rewarding their accomplishments; keeping your mind open and listening to continue learning; and finding happiness by serving.

Sound familiar?

A few of Simmons thoughts: *Don't try to be all things to all people. Nothing usually happens the way it's supposed to.*
Keep yourself open to people.

Simmons had figured out a way to get into my son's head, and did. Already financially successful, and still young, Simmons apparently decided to feed his many followers something of value that they can read and digest.

His book made the NY Times best-seller list.

CHAPTER THIRTY-ONE

THE KEY TO SUCCESS

**You must be willing to risk,
and you must be willing to pay the price.**

There is nothing in this book that you haven't already read or heard somewhere before. And there was nothing that Nightingale, Carnegie, Peale or Simmons wrote that hadn't been written by someone else. Thus, this book has been calculated to save you time, eliminate any anxiety you have previously felt about being rejected and to help you construct your own personal road to your own personal destination.

One of the biggest best sellers in the past few years is: *NATURAL CURES*. The guy who wrote it certainly did his homework by reading everything he could find on the subject, then condensing it into a readable and understandable book.

If you want to live longer and be healthy while here, I highly recommend it. I bought a bunch of them and gave them as gifts to people who I cared about and can read.

The author of "NATURAL CURES" attacks greedy people. I suppose that would be okay if he didn't fall into the same category. He insists that he cares about you, the reader, and wrote the book only to help you become healthy. He then states that there is an alleged natural "CURE" for every disease, but you have to subscribe to his website to find the answer. Sounds like the old "BAIT/SWITCH" to me.

Don't get me wrong. I am a one hundred percent booster of the "NATURAL CURES" book. I just think it's too bad that the author didn't read this book first.

Now let's get back to *THE ABCs OF SUCCESSFULLY SELLING YOURSELF AND IDEAS*. It has not been designed to make you a Donald Trump, Warren Buffet, Bill Gates or Sam Walton. They are exceptions that rose to the zenith of their chosen worlds – maybe born with the Beethoven gift.

The goal of this book is to arm you with the correct ammunition to comfortably travel the road to success. This book's alphabetical aids will be your street signs. If you follow them, you will most certainly succeed.

As Earl Nightingale said so eloquently, "If you set your own goals, write them down and go after them with a positive attitude and self-confidence, there is no way you cannot succeed."

You can go all the way back to Confucius (551 BC – 479 BC) and discover that his musings were the same as you find in all of today's success motivation courses – many advertised on TV for hundreds of dollars by motivators worth millions.

Where do you think they earned their money?

Off you, of course.

How much money do you think Socrates or Plato charged to share their ideas?

How about Confucius?

How often did you read about Jesus passing the plate after one of his sermons?

My case rests!

When someone offers a helping hand I always measure his or her sincerity with the price tag that goes along with it. Maybe that's the true way of measuring a person's heart.

Think about it!

"It's not possible for one to teach others who cannot teach his own family."

Does that sound familiar?

How about: "If you enjoy what you do, you'll never work another day." Socrates (469 BC – 399 BC) said those words.

"All wrongdoing is based on ignorance," He said that, too. So did Russell Simmons.

From the beginning of time, the guideposts have been there. It has been our choice to follow them or not. We have always been in control of our own destiny – and most of us have chosen to be victims. It is always the easiest path.

Do you recall studying Shakespeare in high school?

AS YOU LIKE IT.

"All the world's a stage and we are all just the players in it."

Ever wonder what he meant by that line?

How about this? Life is a play that has already been scripted. Most people get out of bed in the morning and just follow the script (go with the flow). Yet a few, maybe the one in ten, say; "Screw that! No one's going to write my play for me. I'm going to write my own script, star in it, produce it, direct it and even write in the characters that I enjoy being with. I'm going to be in control of my own story."

What do you think?

We can be just another player and follow the script, or we can be the star and write our own.

I like the latter.

The fact that you've read this far says to me that you are ready to prove that you are just as good as anyone else – and you'll never again have to attend an expensive motivation seminar. Why? Because you'll be too busy becoming a success in the field of your choosing – the field of your passion, clicking your heals together and reaching your imaged dream. You will also discover yourself preaching to others (which is okay).

Self-esteem brings that out in all of us.

STRONG SUGGESTION: Make sure you post your written goal in plain sight, preferably in front of you if you are sitting at a desk. Or on the fridge or mirror if you are at home.

I used to carry mine in my pocket because I was constantly on the move. While riding a trolley car (do they still have trolley cars?) I would remove it and stare at it, repeating it over and over. I am sure that the other passengers thought I was nuts.

Don't put it in your desk, notebook, computer or palm pilot. Keep it visibly available – and don't tack it on the wall behind your back.

"YOU BECOME WHAT YOU LOOK AT." You'll see! I hereby give you permission to tack written goals up anywhere in your house that will be visible, or on your office wall. (You should also avail your boss to this book so he won't think you're nuts.)

Don't forget that you also become what you allow to surround you.

Lay down with dogs and get up with fleas. A true cliché!

As a matter of fact, old clichés all come from somewhere for a positive reason. They're usually true and insightful. That's why they survive the test of time.

As preachy as this may seem – you must stay as far away from negative energy as possible. If you choose to travel the success-motivation-highway you must be prepared to announce loud an clear that you cannot allow yourself to be near anyone radiating negative energy. That means that if a negative person wants to continue a friendship with you, they will have to drop all pessimistic discussions and actions in your presence. Don't allow yourself to be anxious about telling them your parameters, the ones they will have to stay within when in your presence. You MUST do this if you decide to control your own life and write your own script. It's for your own protection.

Remember, you cannot help anyone else unless you can help yourself.

Do recovering alcoholics hang around barrooms?

Do recovering dope addicts hang around opium dens?

I don't think so.

You are now a recovering victim, so don't hang around negative energy that is generated by other victims.

Remember, you want to pick your own friends - you don't want them to pick you.

Believe it or not, when you present this ultimatum, your parameters, it will be a service to them. If they value your friendship, they will drop all negatives when you're around. It will be good for their mental health. Or they won't drop all negatives and you'll cease to see them.

Whose loss?

Theirs!

Traveling a new road can be quite lonely at times. You'll find some who will follow you and benefit by your hard work. More power to them! You'll also find old acquaintances that will scoff you and fall by the wayside. When that happens, just remember that you are the writer, producer, director, and star of your own play. Let them go. It is their loss. You can't control their lives. You can only control yours.

You have read that life is made up of moments – many of them – but too few memorable ones. Get ready to add numerous, marvelous, memorable moments to your diary.

It is written in many prudent places that whatever you give will come back ten-fold.

Don't wait any longer!

Write down your goal and go for it.

Take risks.

Give yourself permission to succeed.

Follow the *ALPHABET OF SUCCESSFULLY SELLING YOURSELF AND IDEAS*, and I guarantee that you can have anything and everything that you want.

And, you can take that to the bank!

FINAL EXAM

If I were ever called upon to teach a school course I'd follow the example of one of my teachers when he shocked his students by handing them the questions a week before the exam. He explained, "I just spent an entire semester trying to pound certain information into your thick skulls. If you learn nothing else from this course, it's my fondest wish that you remember this." He then handed out the questions.

Made sense to me.

Why didn't other professors follow suit?

Maybe they'd have to get an okay from the School Board.

The only thing I'd do differently is to hand out the answers and allow the students to supply the questions.

So, here's your final exam, fans. I hope you graduate.

SUPPLY THE QUESTIONS TO THE FOLLOWING ANSWERS. NO CHEATING, PLEASE.

1. See everything through the other person's eyes.
2. Create an atmosphere in which the person you are communicating with will be comfortable doing what you want them to do.

3. There are at least two sides to every story.
4. Write down your goal and keep looking at it. Give it a time limit.
5. Look for the good in others and then comment on it.
6. Image your goal already reached.
7. Stay in control by anticipating all possible answers.
8. Listen to motivation CDs in your car.
9. Concentrate on helping others to be rewarded first, you second. Remember the multi-million dollar Hertz/Avis ad campaign? The company that said they were number two, was actually number one.
10. Take at least one extra step every day.
11. Listen twice as much as you talk.
12. Take responsibility for everything that happens to you.
13. Most answers are found in your own common sense.
14. Learn something new every day.
15. Everything you give will come back ten-fold, but not necessarily from where you gave it.
16. There is no such word as CAN'T.
17. Write your own script.

End of exam!

Don't wait for me to give you a grade.

Give yourself permission to grade it yourself.

Any mark that turns you on. You are now in control – writing your own script. No one is ever again going to rule your life. Not a teacher, a boss, a spouse – but you – the one who should be in control. You will have no one else to blame.

Choose your future. A passion! It is all possible.

Don't be afraid to take risks.

Don't be afraid of giving yourself permission.

Don't be anxious of rejection.

Don't even consider how not to do something. Always look for how to do something.

Above all, don't be afraid to whimper. That was your first sales pitch.

Isn't it too bad we can't find someone to teach this course in high school!

Remember that famous quote on page one? ***"Life might not be the party we hoped for, but while we're here we might as well dance."***

After reading this book I guarantee that you won't hesitate to ask that cutie if you can be added to her or his dance card.

RECOMMENDED READING:

HOW TO WIN FRIENDS AND INFLUENCE PEOPLE
Written by Dale Carnegie
Published by Pocket Books, a division of Simon and Schuster, copyright 1936.

THE HOLY BIBLE
Written by?

THE POWER OF POSITIVE THINKING
Written by Dr. Norman Vincent Peale
Published by Random House, NY, NY

THE ESSENCE OF SUCCESS
Written by Earl Nightingale
Published by Nightingale-Conant Corp,

THE ALPHABET TO SUCCESSFULLY SELLING YOURSELF AND IDEAS
Written by Roland Hopkins
AuthorHouse

LIFE AND DEF, SEX, DRUGS, MONEY AND GOD
Written by Russell Simmons
Crown Publishing

About the Author

Roland Hopkins was born 1936 in Boston, spent his youth, education and business career in good-old-handshake, Yankee New England. His first paying job was as a soda jerk on old Cape Cod, he then worked as an archery instructor in Maine, he attended college in Connecticut, spent six years as a disc jockey in Connecticut and Maine, married a girl from Vermont and then founded a small business newspaper in Boston. Early in his career he discovered two things that rules his life. ONE – He decided that he would never become a salesperson. TWO – When he did become a salesperson, a respected and successful business friend executive informed him that you can never become successful in business following the Golden Rule – Do Unto Others. Apparently it was a challenge that Roland accepted because his small, 12-page weekly business newspaper, started on a shoestring, became the largest commercial real estate newspaper in the country by following the very philosophy that he was advised would never work.

Roland is married to Denise, a former horserace jockey who was the first woman to win a riding title at a major race track and ultimately won over a thousand races. He has four children, all successful in varied fields – Kathi, a graduate of the University of New Hampshire; Tracey, a graduate of the University of Rhode Island; Rock who attended the University of Vermont; and Stephen who attended New England College.

Roland lives on a horse farm in Vermont for 6 months, and a horse farm in Florida for 6 months. He is also the published author of a very exciting noir mystery novel that can be found on Amazon.

Printed in the United States
210937BV00001B/189/A

9 781434 348821